NEW WORLD ORDER

THE RISE OF TRANSNATIONAL CORPORATE REPUBLIC

NEW WORLD ORDER

THE RISE OF TRANSNATIONAL CORPORATE REPUBLIC

Balvinder Ruby

New World Order
The Rise of Transnational Corporate Republic
Balvinder Ruby

All rights reserved
Second Edition, 2025
© Balvinder Ruby, 2025

No part of this publication may be reproduced, or stored in a retrieval system, or transmitted in any form by means of electronic, mechanical, photocopying or otherwise, without prior written permission from the publisher.

The views expressed in this work are solely those of the author and do not reflect the views of the publisher, and the publisher hereby disclaims any responsibility for them.

Requests for permission should be addressed to the publisher.

ISBN - 978-1-7641296-1-91-9

 A Catalogue for this book is available from the National Library of Australia

Disclaimer: The author and publisher take no responsibility for any errors, omissions, or contradictions that may exist in the book

Contents

Preface ix
Acknowledgements xi
List of Illustrations xiii
1   **Introduction** 1
2   **Conspiracy Theories**..6
3   **Demise of the Democracies** 11
        3.1   Background 11
        3.2   Case Studies 15
        3.3   De-legitimation of Democracy - Electoral Frauds 17
              3.3.1 Lure of Cash and Drugs to Entice Voters 17
              3.3.2 Criminals as Lawmakers 19
              3.3.3 Election Funding, a Corporate Connection....20
              3.3.4 Legalisation of Corruption-Electoral Bonds ...20
        3.4   Media...24
              3.4.1 Social Media 24
              3.4.2 Fake News..28
              3.4.3 Polarisation of Society 33
              3.4.4 Muzzling the Media..33
              3.4.5 Media Monopolies 34
        3.5   Political Infirmities...39
              3.5.1 Political Correctness......................................39
              3.5.2 Opinion Surveys 40
              3.5.3 Identity Politics...41
              3.5.4 Post-Truth and Demagoguery 42
        3.6   Self-Immolation of Democracy - Right-Wing Extremism 44

4	**Incapacitation of Capitalism**	...47
	4.1 Background	...47
	4.2 What is Capitalism?	...49
	4.2.1 Non-Performing Assets (NPA) - the Cancer of Capitalism	...52
	4.2.2 Gross Domestic Product (GDP) - Growth For the Sake of Growth is a Contagion	...55
	4.2.3 Shock Doctrine	...58
	4.2.4 Stock Market	...59
	4.2.5 Delusion of shareholders	...62
	4.3 Behind the Corporate Veil	...63
	4.3.1 Shell Companies	...64
	4.3.2 Money Laundering	...65
	4.3.3 Black Money	...68
	4.3.4 Corporate Bailouts	...68
	4.4 Bretton Wood and the Economic theory - the formation of the World Bank and International Monetary Fund (IMF)	...70
	4.5 World Economic Forum (WEF)	...72
	4.6 Indebtedness, a Political Weapon	...73
	4.7 Climate Bogey, a Ploy to Bolster Corporations	...77
	4.8 COVID-19 Pandemic-a boon for the billionaire	...81
5	**Metamorphosis of the Monetary System**	...86
	5.1 Background	...86
	5.2 The Money	...87
	5.3 Digital Currency	...88
	5.4 Cryptocurrency	...89
	5.5 Non-Fungible Tokens	...90

	5.6	Crypto Exchanges 91
	5.7	Blockchain, the Technology 93
	5.8	Cryptocurrency Currency-End of Monetary Sovereignty 96
6	**Negation of Nation-States** **99**	
	6.1	Globalisation 99
	6.2	Dilution of Sovereignty 103
	6.3	Dual Citizenship 103
	6.4	Corporate Citizenship 105
	6.5	Citizenship for Sale 107
	6.6	Chinese Debt-Trap Diplomacy 110
7	**The Rise of Transnational Corporate Republic** **114**	
	7.1	Tax Havens 114
	7.2	Corporate State 117
	7.3	Corporatocracy 121
	7.4	State Corporation 126
	7.5	Transnational Corporate Republic 129
8	**Conclusions** **135**	
Notes **137**		
Bibliography **146**		
About the Author **156**		
Also by Balvinder Ruby **157**		

Preface

This book makes an effort to examine and comprehend the post-World war political, economic, and strategic developments that resulted in the transfer of power from the United Kingdom to the United States of America. Two parallel politico-economic and ideological models emerged and prevailed during the Cold War era, the liberal democratic capitalistic model led by the US and the communist, socialist model led by the erstwhile Union of Soviet Socialist Republic (USSR) confronting each other as ideological and military rivals through alliances NATO and Warsaw Pact maintaining a balance of power. Though a third Non-Aligned Movement (NAM) bloc also played a role to some extent in maintaining the power balance, The fall and disintegration of the USSR led to a unipolar world with the US at the helm of affairs as the sole arbitrator of geopolitical and economic order at the global level.

In their bid to seek markets in third-world countries for their products, the US and other western countries conceptualised and promoted the idea of globalisation. Globalisation resulted in two unintended consequences. Firstly, the manufacturing moved largely to China, making it a global manufacturing hub; secondly, the services industry shifted to Third World countries like India, made possible by the model of outsourcing and advances in information technology and telecommunications. Losing the manufacturing and services sectors weakened the West's and the US's hegemonic dominance. As a result, the US no longer remains the sole superpower, as China has caught up with it in terms of economic power.

When the global supply chain from China broke down during the COVID-19 pandemic, it became painfully clear that the world depended on China for almost all manufactured goods. In this changing scenario, transnational corporations try to reap benefits and grow their clout by strategically shifting their manufacturing and marketing bases.

The primary purpose of this book is to understand how this new dynamic will pan out against the backdrop of the gradual decline of the democratic model of governance over time and how the insidious rise of transnational corporations in power is going to reshape the emerging new world order.

Acknowledgements

I would like to express my special gratitude, appreciation, and thanks to my all-time mentor, initiator, trainer, supervisor, colleague, and friend, Dr ON Bhargava, Emeritus Professor, Punjab University, Chandigarh, India; Former Visiting Professor, Vienna University; Former Director, Geological Survey of India; and INSA Honorary Scientist at Indian National Science Academy, who has always been a source of inspiration and motivation. I am highly indebted to him for instilling a keen sense of inquiry and scientific temperament.

My special thanks are due to Dr KC Prashra, former director of the Geological Survey of India and an eminent scientist and poet, who initiated me into the world of publishing and helped me publish many research papers in different scientific journals.

I'd like to thank many smart and wise friends, in particular, with whom I've had the chance to talk for a long time about many different topics and have many brainstorming sessions. These discussions facilitated the subject of the book and helped me develop, refine, and fine-tune the concepts, and provided me with additional meaningful inputs on various counts to add value to my ideas. In this context, I'd like to specifically call out the names of Jiwan Dhillon, a former director of estimates coordination at the Defence Materials Organisation in Canberra, Australian Capital Territory, Dr Dalbir Ahlawat, a senior lecturer in the department of security studies and criminology at Macquarie University in

Australia and Rawender Guron, a former database administrator at RTA in NSW, Australia.

I would particularly like to place on record the assistance received from Jiwan Dhillon, who critically went through and reviewed the script and suggested numerous improvements that helped improve the context, content and quality.

I would like to express my gratitude, love and affection to my eleven years granddaughter Samreen and seven-year grandson Johar, who are the pillars of my strength and keep me energised and recharged by heaps of their innocent and contagious smiles and hugs.

Balvinder Ruby
Sydney, February 2023

List of Illustrations

Figure 1: Cold War and the bipolar world 2

Figure 2: A bizarre conspiracy theory puts Bill Gates at the centre of the coronavirus crisis. 9

Figure 3: List of countries by system of government 12

Figure 4: Parliament (Lok Sabha) election 2019: The seizure of cash, drugs/narcotics, gold, and other valuables has already crossed the figures of the 2014 Lok Sabha election. (Photo: ANI) 17

Figure 5: Comparison of seizure of drugs, cash and liquor (2014 vs 2019) 18

Figure 6: Electoral Bonds 22

Figure 7: Social Media 25

Figure 8: Top 15 Social media sites with active users in millions 26

Figure 9: Fake news 28

Figure 10: Media ownership US 35

Figure 11: Who owns the media? 37

Figure 12: Media Interests snapshot, Australia 38

Figure 13: Shareholders of 22 companies grew $1.5 trillion richer, while workers got less than two per cent of the benefit 54

Figure 14: Global Fortune 500 growth vs global GDP growth 2009-19 55

Figure 15: What is Gross Domestic Product, and how does it affect you? 57

Figure 16: Stock Market Index 60

Figure 17: The World's biggest tax havens 66

Figure 18: Money Laundering Cycle 67

Figure 19: Pathology of bad debts 69

Figure 20: List of countries by negative Net International
Investment Position (Debtors)..74

Figure 21: List of countries by positive Net International
Investment Position (Creditors) 75

Figure 22: Continental Drift 78

Figure 23: Carbon marketing..81

Figure 24: COVID-19 Gainers 82

Figure 25: Global COVID-19 pandemic-opportunities
for the big pharma industry 84

Figure 26: Centralised and Decentralised 91

Figure 27: Popular cryptocurrencies as of June 3. 2022
Popular Cryptocurrencies as of June 3, 2022..........................92

Figure 28: The properties of Distributed
Ledger Technology 93

Figure 29: Distributed Autonomous Organisation...................................94

Figure 30: Millionaire migration 108

Figure 31: Chinese Debt-trap diplomacy...110

Figure 32: Mapping the Belt and Road Initiative 111

Figure 33: Global Economic Shift...130

1 Introduction

Understanding the post-World War II political, economic, social, and technological developments can open a window into how those forces will manifest themselves in reshaping and realigning the world order. The Post-Cold War era resulted in the dismembering of the then mighty empire, the Union of Soviet Socialist Republic, that led to a unipolar world with the US at the helm of affairs as the sole arbitrator of political and economic and military power. Now, the towering position of the US as a world leader seems to be increasingly challenged as a result of the unintended consequences of globalisation. This makes it intriguing to watch the world order change and a new one emerge and to make predictions about where this might take us.

Two parallel socio-economic and ideological models were in existence. They prevailed during the Cold War era stretching between March 12, 1947, and December 26, 1991, the liberal democratic capitalist model led by the US and the communist, socialist model led by the erstwhile Union of Socialist Soviet Republic (USSR) confronting each other as ideological and military rivals through alliances. The US-led capitalist group of countries formed NATO in 1949, followed by the declaration of the Warsaw Pact in 1955 by the USSR-led communist group of countries. The Warsaw Pact was formally the Treaty of Friendship, Cooperation, and Mutual Assistance, a form of a collective defence treaty signed in Warsaw, Poland, between the Soviet Union and seven other Eastern Bloc socialist republics of Central and Eastern Europe. These blocs attempted to manoeuvre one another by engaging in a proxy war, sabotage, and intrigue while also engaging in a nuclear arms race, media manipulation, and a race for space. It was mainly a bipolar world, and the balance of power was maintained by them checking on each other. A third bloc, the Non-Aligned Movement (NAM), an initiative of Josip Broz Tito, the president of then Yugoslavia; Jawahar Lal Nehru, Prime Minister of India; Gamal Abdel Nasar, President of Egypt; Kwame Nkrumah, President of Ghana; and Sukarno, President of Indonesia, also played a significant role in maintaining the balance of power.

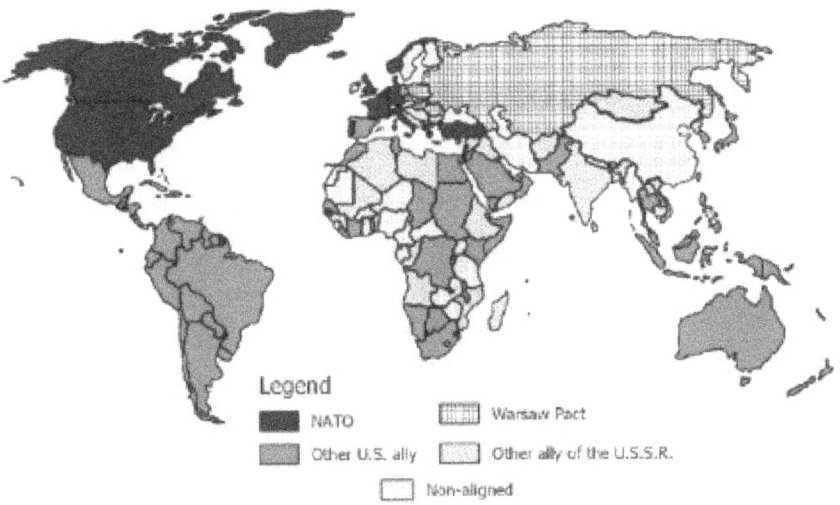

Figure 1: Cold War and the bipolar world

Source: Joseph Salukvadze; https://www.researchgate.net/profile/Joseph-Salukvadze/publication/329844941/figure/fig1/AS:706387063611397@1545427208947/Cold-War-and-the-bipolar-world_W640.jpg

Nuclear power served as a deterrent for both of these blocs after the USSR developed it in 1949, as they accumulated their firepower to a level of mutually assured destruction.

The US and USSR played violent havoc on either side through third-party proxy wars, government or militia financing, and providing arms, training and logistical support. Several incidents of proxy wars that took place during the Cold War era include the erection of the Berlin Wall, the Korean War, the Arab-Israeli War, the Cuban Missile Crisis, the Angola War, the Vietnam War (1962-1975) and the military intervention (1979-1989).

The collapse and disintegration of the USSR (16 November 1988–26 December 1991) proved that the communist socio-economic model did not stand the test of time. With the fall of the USSR, the US assumed a more aggressive and belligerent role in the absence of a counterbalance and freely engaged in military drills abroad without concern for or hostility toward retaliation.

In the past, under the guise of thwarting the Soviet threat during the Cold War, the US intervened in third-world nations. In the post-Cold War era, it changed its stance from protecting countries from the USSR to enforcing peace and acting as a global policeman. It even went beyond that facade and supported totalitarian regimes under this guise. Not only that, it used this pretext to legitimise its refusal to negotiate the American withdrawal from Kuwait in the Gulf War (Northcott, Michael S, 1993). In its efforts to maintain and legitimise its military interests, overt or covert, it needed new enemies in the absence of the USSR and found Colonel Gaddafi of Libya, Fidel Castro of Cuba, the Ayatollah in Iran and then Saddam Hussein in Iraq and so on. Its action in Iraq was a classic example of its obnoxious attitude and aggressiveness with the bogey of weapons of mass destruction. Its doublespeak becomes evident when it chooses to stay away from North Korea, which openly claims to have such weapons.

It seems the US did not learn anything from its humiliating defeat and exit from Vietnam in 1973. The US eventually became mired in a protracted quagmire and decided to withdraw from Afghanistan on May 1, 2021. This was a blow to the capitalistic model and an indication that this model, too, is neither ideal nor practicable in the long run.

The free market capitalist model of the liberal democratic bloc has repeatedly suffered severe reverses in recent decades. As such, capitalism in its pure form does not exist anywhere in the world. Regular and blatant corporate bailouts undermine the fundamental principles of the free market dynamics model and serve as a sign that capitalism has failed and is falling prey to the growing corporate powers. In most so-called democratic capitalist countries, the presence of numerous social security schemes is the antithesis of the capitalist model.

The formation of the World Trade Organisation (WTO), the signing of Free Trade Agreements and the setting up of Special Economic Zones facilitated by the advancements in technology, telecommunications, and the Internet, have accelerated the dilution of the sovereign state concept because of the free flow of goods, services, capital, and human resources across the world.

The current monetary system of the Treasury, banks, and fiat currencies has been challenged by technological advancements and the appearance of cryptocurrency on the horizon. There are signs that cryptocurrency may soon replace the current monetary system. All the traditional trade and commerce processes will move on to blockchain technology. Blockchain is also the platform for the first-ever cryptocurrency, Bitcoin, which started in 2009.

The shareholder-centric stock market, which promotes monopolistic practices, tax havens, mergers, and shell company structures, has completely corrupted capitalism, abandoned the state, and given corrupt politicians and multinational corporations the perfect platform to carry out their nefarious schemes to be the saving friends of capitalists and amass wealth. As a result, corporations grew extremely powerful, taking control of the world economy and even starting to impose their will on governments. The idea of sovereign states is being diluted by this trend, which could ultimately result in their extinction.

These changes are taking place at a fast pace, and corporations are virtually taking over the reins from governments, reducing the heads of state to mere pawns in the corporate chess game. Numerous politicians, after retirement, are employed by corporations as advisors or lobbyists.

Last but not least, the terrifying development that seems to be developing is that the Chinese State, which is neither socialist nor capitalist but rather a hybrid of the two—practically an ideal cocktail mix—is assuming the role of a corporation, the mightiest one, and has made significant investments in far too many nations through its belt and road initiative. Its other more sinister behind-the-scenes moves are yet to be noticed, like influencing politicians of all hues in all countries and getting people with a soft heart for Chinese interests to get into parliaments worldwide. For example, Sam Dastyari, an Australian Labor Party frontbencher, had to quit politics on charges of acting under the influence of the Chinese Government. Under Xi Jinping, the Chinese government has gone into overdrive to influence foreign countries (Murali, A.G.A.C.I.V.S., (2017, November 30). China's efforts to influence foreign politicians have been well documented (Chubb, A, 2022) since 2000.

2 Conspiracy Theories

The New World Order has been the subject of scrutiny and shrouded with many notorious but vague conspiracy theories. According to these theories, it is claimed that some powerful group of individuals is either secretly running the world, conspiring to do so, or on the verge of gaining such control.

This conspiracy theory continues to exist because prominent political figures occasionally bring it up in another context to emphasise their point. On January 29th 1991, US President George H W Bush, in his second State of the Union address, while speaking when the Gulf War was well underway in his zeal to promote the new era, claimed the conflict represented.

> "A big idea, a new world order, where diverse nations are drawn together in common cause to achieve the universal aspirations of mankind - peace and security, freedom, and the rule of law. Such is a world worthy of our struggle and worthy of our children's future." – George H W Bush

A conspiracy is a dubious agenda that a person, a group of people, or a body politic concocts to accomplish maliciously in order to obtain the intended result for their hidden ulterior goal from the knowledge of the general public. It is disguised, packed in what appears to be innocent and lofty language, and presented in a way that makes it seem as though it is pursuing higher principles and social justice for the benefit of regular people.

At the same time, on the other hand, a genuine concept, idea, or concern may be branded as malicious and conspiracy by those very persons, a group of persons, or a body politic, as their interests will be harmed by this new phenomenon.

By default, a conspiracy theory is just a conjecture, not real, hard facts and untrue. Over time, new data and corroborating facts may establish it as a factual scenario. If and when that time comes, the theory is established and proven.

Conspiracy theories ordinarily consist of three interconnected elements, their goals are nefarious, their actions are sly or manipulative, and the conspirators have the ability to work around them, given their powerful position to control the course of events and the narrative. Lastly, they operate in secrecy and cover up their real activities. The cover-up may involve the fabrication of data, the removal of the evidence, or the influencing of the persons who control the official narrative. Anyone whose job is to question everything, like the media and academia, and who espouses scepticism or contempt toward the official narrative is despised, frowned upon, and dubbed as anti-people or anti-national.

The common theme of the conspiracy about a New World Order is that a secretive elite with a globalist agenda is conspiring to eventually take over and rule the world, potentially destroying and replacing sovereign nation-states.

Historically, many contemporary influential figures have been alleged to be part of such an obnoxious cabal that envisages operating through front organisations in a bid to orchestrate significant political and financial events. They manufacture systemic and planned crises to push through controversial national and international policies as part of their design in an ongoing plot to achieve world dominance.

According to Stephen O'Leary, a professor at the University of Southern California's Annenberg School who has spent two decades researching conspiracy theories, those who support them believe that a new era of international cooperation between various countries and cultures is on the horizon that will enable all of the planet's inhabitants to have access to everything they require. Conversely, the detractors claim that it is a systematic approach to take-over by a combination of quasi-government entities and corporations that are hell-bent on covertly taking over and organising an all-powerful global government aiming to regulate every aspect of citizens' lives, reducing them to a perpetual working class.

This conspiracy theory is credited to right-wing anti-government extremists from the 1990s onward who think that a socialist tyrannical one-world conspiracy has already seized control of most of the world, according to conspiracy theory expert Mark Dice. With the aid of accomplices within the government, it intends to put an end to the free society through repressive measures and manufactured crises like terrorist attacks and pandemics to put an end to dissent.

Anne-Marie Slaughter approaches this topic entirely differently and urges us to reconsider how we perceive politics. According to her, it is not a collection of nation-states that communicate through heads of government like presidents, prime ministers, foreign ministers, and the United Nations or NGOs, but it is governance through a web of government networks.

Slaughter insists that global governance is here--but not where most people think, as the government officials, police investigators, financial regulators, judges and even legislators exchange information and coordinate activity across national borders to tackle crime and terrorism on a routine basis as part of international interactions.

Great Reset, an initiative of the World Economic Forum launched in June 2020, calls for an apparently fairer outcome and a rethinking of global investment and government expenditure to revive the world economy after the devastation caused by the COVID-19 epidemic.

Figure 2: A bizarre conspiracy theory puts Bill Gates at the centre of the coronavirus crisis.
Source: https://shorturl.at/dsuJT

This initiative has refuelled the New World Order conspiracy theory. It is thought to be a renewed conspiracy to bring about a one-world government by the elite group under cover of COVID-19 to use it as an opportunity to enable forced vaccination, taking away privacy, the introduction of digital IDs and renunciation of property rights by the public. For example, Bill Gates has become the centre of a bizarre conspiracy theory during the coronavirus crisis because of his prediction of such pandemics and his commercial involvement and interests in the business of vaccines.

This conspiracy theory has so far been discussed in a hushed tone for a long time, but it has come to the surface now and has become a really big issue of the current times. The chairman of the World Economic Forum (WEF), Klaus Schwab, has long pushed for such a possibility and promoted the notion that multinational corporations (also known as "transnational corporations") should go beyond simply serving their shareholders and take on additional responsibilities such as serving as stewards of society. He is suggesting and emphasising that transnational corporations should take on the responsibility of governing the world, and this malicious and sinister design of giving power over societies to the corporations stands exposed now.

It is interesting to note that the stakeholders in this holdup include the world's biggest corporations and their scope of operations. These corporations are from different sectors, such as Audi, Aramco, Shell, Chevron, and BP from the oil industry; Unilever; The Coca-Cola Company, and Nestlé from food; Facebook, Google, Amazon, Microsoft, and Apple from technology and AstraZeneca, Pfizer, and Moderna from pharmaceuticals. It is clear from a cursory glance at these names who they are and what they are up to.

In this scenario, governments can be relegated to being one of the many simple stakeholders. At the same time, it promoted corporations as the official decision-makers and stakeholders. These developments have challenged the concept of democracy discussed in the next chapter.

3 Demise of the Democracies

3.1 Background

The term "democracy" has its origin in Greek because, in the mid-fifth century, such a political system existed in Athens and some other adjoining cities in the area. The English word "democracy" is derived from the Greek word "demokratia," where "demos" stands for the people and "kratos" for authority or control. The concept of nation-states as such did not exist at that time. Since then, the theory and practices of democracy have evolved considerably as new ideas have flowed over time, resulting in the formation of nation-states and sovereign states in the early eighteenth century. Many countries, particularly in Northern Europe and America, embraced democracy as a model for their political system.

Ideally, in a democracy, people should directly participate in framing policies. But because of the large number of people in a particular country, it becomes impractical and impossible to work it out that way. People in a specified area can choose their representative to overcome this limitation. The representatives thus elected from different constituencies/areas of different parties participate in the decision-making process to formulate policies for the public good. This type of democracy is called a representative democracy. The essential characteristic of democracy is freedom of assembly, association, speech, equality, and liberty of individual citizens.

Theoretically, there are many types of democracies, but in reality, there are only two forms of democracy in the world currently, the presidential form of democracy and the parliamentary form of democracy.

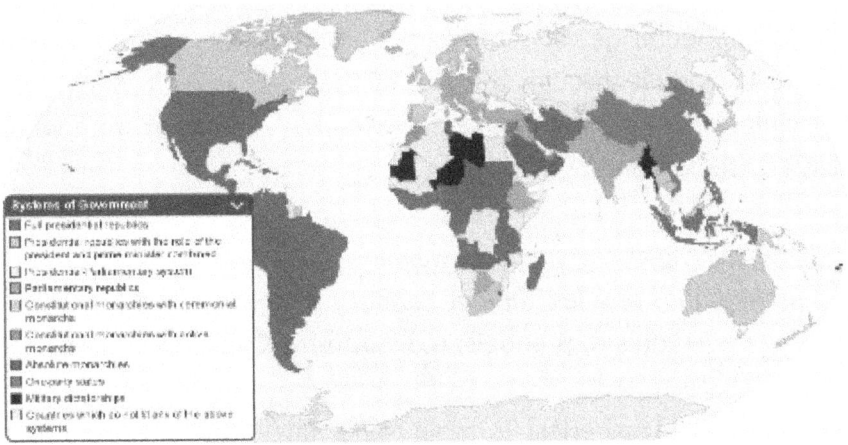

Figure 3: List of countries by system of government
Source: https://i.redd.it/ivqt3um9ehd21.jpg

Parliamentary democracy is a system where the executive derives its power from the parliament, to which it is accountable. In this system, the head of the state is distinct from the head of the government. The head of the cabinet committee is the head of government. The parliament system of democracy is the dominant form of government in the world, as it is practised in thirty-two out of fifty sovereign states in Europe (Figure 1). Additionally, ten of the thirteen Caribbean islands, Australia, and New Zealand also practise it. This system is also followed in erstwhile British colonies, including India.

A presidential form of government is a single executive system where the "President" is the head of the state and the government. In a presidential system, the president is directly elected by the populace and is not answerable to the legislature. Nineteen of the twenty-two sovereign states in North and South America, with the exception of Canada, Belize, and Suriname, have this type of structure. This technique is also used in Central Asia and Southern and Central Africa.

The fundamental idea of democracy is, in theory, the empowerment of the individual through the use of the "one person, one vote" principle. However, the reality is substantially different from what was envisioned on the ground.

> *"We may have democracy, or we may have wealth concentrated in the hands of a few, but we cannot have both."*
> – Louis D. Brandeis, U.S. Supreme Court, 1916-1939

Individuals are powerless in reality and have little to no input in the decision-making process as a result of several malpractices that have gradually crept in over time and reduced them to nothing more than a number, a vote. This erosion in the importance of the individuals, making them meek, weak, vulnerable, and helpless in actual practice, is one of the main reasons for democracy falling from grace, losing its relevance, and decaying. The other major reason behind corporations usurping power is that politicians hand over governance to corporations on a platter.

> *"Aristotle's objection to democracy was that it was inherently unstable. It transmuted naturally into tyranny. It is not law or constitutions that have prevented this from happening in the century and a half during which democracy has been the prevailing system in Europe and North America. It is a shared political culture. Like most cultural phenomena, shared political culture is spontaneous growth. It is difficult to create. But it is very easy to destroy."*
> – Jonathan Sumption (Sumption, Jonathan., 2021).

Simply put, democracies are under attack all over the world because leaders are pursuing populist policies at the expense of pluralism and securing unchecked power at the expense of minorities by portraying minorities as perceived enemies. The leaders seem to be indulging in such unethical and insidious practices to retain power forever by generating fear psychosis by creating such bogeys, leading to the setting up of people against people for their authoritarian and dictatorial designs. The situation is equally bad in most democracies.

These authoritarian leaders are getting bolder and bolder each year. The number of countries with declining political rights and civil liberties is consistently growing. The world's oldest and biggest democracies, the United States of America and India, are particularly notable for this. In India, since taking over in 2014, the Hindu Nationalist government, headed by Narinder Modi, has been pressurising and strangulating human rights organisations, intimidating civil liberties groups, academicians, and journals with a spate of bigoted attacks like the lynching of ethnic minority Muslims.

Because of the COVID-19 epidemic, authoritarian leaders were able to abuse their power and restrict civil liberties and dissent. They did this by spreading false information and propaganda, forcing the media to do what they wanted, and often shutting down the internet and mobile networks.

The democratically elected leaders are perpetrating democratic decay in small steps by employing seemingly legal mechanisms. This is done by impairing the ability of the opposition leaders to question, disqualify, and harass them, weakening the democratic institutions by bringing about changes through legal channels, crippling or blocking the media, and impairing free and fair elections. This is also accomplished by undermining the rule of law by overseeing the judicial system and luring judges with lucrative post-retirement positions or by nominating them to the parliament's Upper House.

3.2 Case Studies

For the sake of convenience, I have chosen India, the biggest democracy, Australia, the youngest democracy, and the United States, the oldest democracy, as case studies to compare and contrast the democratic systems to illustrate and demonstrate my point. Though India and Australia both have parliamentary democracies where the national governments are elected by secret ballot, with Australia being a constitutional monarchy while India is a constitutional republic, there are some significant differences worth mentioning.

The first significant difference is that voting is voluntary in India, whereas it is compulsory in Australia and enforced through fines for not voting. Moreover, India has recently introduced the option to vote for none of the candidates, or NOTA, which stands for "none of the above." India is using electronic voting machines, while the rest of the world has abandoned these after trying them, finding them unsuitable because of the possibilities of manipulation. Numerous claims of electronic voting system manipulation in recent elections have surfaced in India.

Secondly, Australia has a preferential voting system where the voters are required to indicate their first preference by placing one against a candidate's name, then make a second preference, and so on for the number of candidates on the ballot paper. If no candidate gets an absolute majority of the first preference votes, then the candidate with the fewest votes is eliminated, and those votes are allocated to the other candidates according to the number of second preference votes. If still no majority is reached, the process is repeated, with the candidate getting the least votes. This type of voting is confusing, cumbersome and lengthy, but it is the best system because, in this system, the winning candidate is the most preferred. Moreover, the votes of other minor parties also get counted towards deciding the winner. The parties sharing overlapping philosophies and policies can assist each other by allocating their preferences in favour of their party or candidate.

On the other hand, there is no preferential voting system in India. Any party can come into power even with less than fifty per cent of the votes, there being a multi-party system as the votes get divided. For example, the Bharatiya Janata Party in India got into power in 1999 by obtaining only 37.36% of votes, even though 62.64 per cent of the population did not support it. In such a situation, democracy is just a facade.

Thirdly, in Australia, the elections are partly public-funded as the candidates with a certain percentage of votes are reimbursed per vote. In contrast, elections in India are extremely expensive, dependent on illegal funding, and rigged in favour of the party financiers, making the system vulnerable to fraud, corruption, and unethical behaviour.

The US, on the other hand, has a presidential system. The major difference between the presidential and parliamentary systems is the accountability of the executive to the legislature. In a presidential system, the head of government leads an executive independent of the legislature. The head of the government and the head of the state are one and the same person; the President and the executive are not responsible to the legislature.

3.3 De-legitimation of Democracy - Electoral Frauds

3.3.1 Lure of Cash and Drugs to Entice Voters

Figure 4: Parliament (Lok Sabha) election 2019: The seizure of cash, drugs/narcotics, gold, and other valuables has already crossed the figures of the 2014 Lok Sabha election. (Photo: ANI)

Elections form an essential mechanism in representative democracies to elect the legislature after a fixed, regular interval of a few years, depending on the term of the parliament of that particular country. Free and fair elections are paramount and a prerequisite of a healthy and functional democracy.

I have selected India as a case study where the distribution of drugs, money, and alcohol has been a common practice to lure voters. In the 2019 Parliament, (Lok Sabha) elections, goods and cash worth US$ 502 million were seized by the Election Commission, which monitors and uploads daily reports of these seizures (Figure 3).

The comparison between the 2014 and 2019 figures reveals that these numbers continue to rise with each succeeding election (figure-3), despite the numerous official reports and allegations of widespread electoral fraud, manipulation, and violence in India. There is a dearth of academic research on this subject.

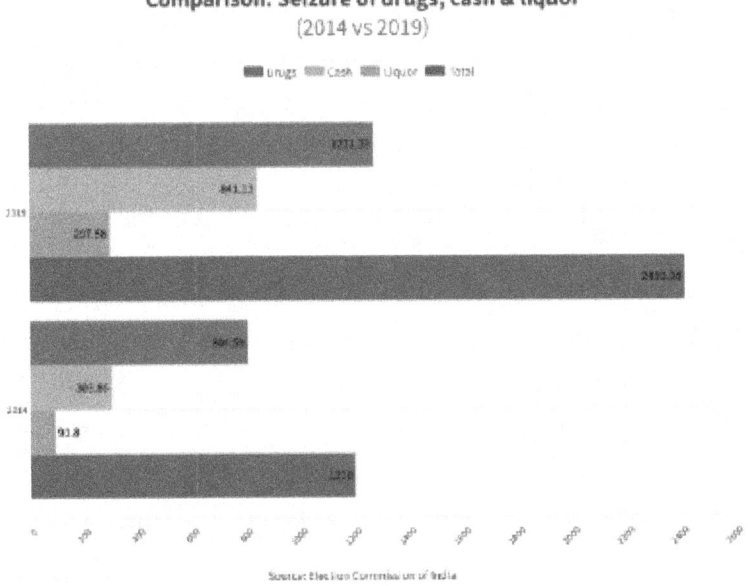

Figure 5: Comparison of seizure of drugs, cash and liquor (2014 vs 2019)
Source: Election Commission of India

Even though it frequently happens in India during state and national elections, this practice is forbidden. There appears to be a lack of political will to uphold the legislation intended to stop this activity. According to a study carried out by Anirban Mitra and Shabana Mitra (Mitra, S., Mitra, A., & MukherJI, A., 2016, January 1), no change in the spending and consumption pattern of households was noticed. Therefore it is hard to say that the distribution of cash, alcohol or drugs by the political parties actually gets translated into more votes.

A report of the Electoral Commission of India on the 2014 national elections states that over seventy-five thousand FIRs in connection with various kinds of poll-related violations were lodged with the police; a huge amount of cash, alcohol, and drugs were seized

(Anon., 2014, May 18). To be precise, over three billion rupees in cash, six and a half million litres of alcohol, and about five hundred thousand kilos of drugs. Vernacular and national media were awash with a wide variety of fraudulent electoral practices. For example, two hundred thousand names mysteriously disappeared from the polling lists in Mumbai. A similar trend was noticed in the 2019 Indian national elections (Martin, N., & Picherit, D., 2019).

3.3.2 Criminals as Lawmakers

An analysis of 8,070 contestants in the 2009 parliament elections from 543 constituencies revealed that wealthy candidates with criminal backgrounds had better chances of winning the election despite having criminal charges laid against them (Duraisamy, P., & Jérôme, B., 2017). Therefore it shows a strong association between wealthy criminal backgrounds and electoral outcomes.

According to the NGO, the Associations of Democratic Reforms (ADR), out of the 259 members elected in the 2019 Parliament elections in India, 233, forming about 43%, have criminal charges against them. There is a 24% increase in these figures compared to the previous elections in 2014.

Many politicians with criminal backgrounds in the parliaments are indicative of the alarming unholy and pervasive alliance between the politicians and the criminals. It is no surprise that criminals are being aided and abetted by politicians (Anup, C., 2020). Milan Vaishnav, in his book, 'When Crime Pays: Money and Muscle in Indian Politics' raises many questions and ask how can free and fair democratic processes co-exist with such a symbiotic relationship between crime and politics (Vaishnav, M., 2017, January 24), with one-third of state and national legislators having repeated criminal backgrounds. The insight of this book brings about one bitter truth: the criminals are elected not because voters are unaware of this information but because of a non-functional judicial system where the criminals provide quick fixes.

3.3.3 Election Funding, a Corporate Connection

Elections are becoming increasingly expensive in democracies that must take place every few years as a part of the political process. All political parties must run in elections, which requires significant financial resources.

What is the source of this funding? The corporations that have access to enormous amounts of money fund the government and opposition parties. What is the purpose of the funding provided by big firms, and what do they expect in return from politicians? They influence politicians to create policies that work for them.

Whom are the politicians supposed to represent in such a situation? Whose interests they are supposed to serve, their masters, the corporations, not the subjects, the citizens. As a result, politicians become nothing more than corporate pawns, forfeit their freedom to express their free will and intellect, and mortgage their consciences to their corporate overlords. They don't have a choice, do they?

An economy is a collection of interconnected activities that include the production, consumption, and distribution of commodities and services to meet people's needs. When we sift through the headlines, we see that the nations are essentially considered economies, with their citizens serving as mere consumers for whatever nonsense the companies continue to spout.

3.3.4 Legalisation of Corruption-Electoral Bonds

India announced the introduction of electoral bonds in January 2018, together with the Finance Bill (2017). Financial tools called electoral bonds are used to give money to political parties. These take the form of promissory notes with a bearer. The holder of the instrument is assumed to be the owner, even though it has neither the name of the buyer nor the payee. In other words, these bonds function exactly like bills of exchange.

Political parties are not permitted to accept donations from foreign organisations, and the Delhi High Court found two significant parties guilty of breaking the Foreign Contributions (Regulations) Act (FCRA) of 1976 in 2014 by illegally accepting funds from two companies that were registered in India but whose controlling shareholder was a foreign corporation. The current BJP government revised the FRCA retroactively in 2016 and 2018 through the Finance Bills and established the Electoral Bonds, guaranteeing complete anonymity for the businesses. Nothing less than legalising corruption and money laundering is being attempted here. Theoretically, the political parties can now be fully funded by a foreign company operating in India through a shell company. Moreover, only profit-making companies could make political donations earlier, but now even loss-making companies can donate.

The State Bank of India may issue electoral bonds in multiples of Rs 1,000, Rs 10,000, Rs 100,000, and Rs 10,000,000. (one crore). Any Indian national or firm with Indian incorporation may purchase it and give the proceeds to any political party recognised under Section 29A of the Representation of the Peoples Act, 1951 (43 of 1951). Electoral bonds may be received by any registered political party with at least 1% of the votes cast in the most recent general or assembly election. The quantity of bonds that may be purchased is unlimited. The political parties that receive bond donations are not required to preserve any records of the donors' identities or notify India's Election Commissioner. The party's verified account is how the receiver can cash the bonds.

According to the government, the electoral bonds will ensure that all contributions made to a party are recorded in the balance sheets without disclosing the donor's identity, allowing for monitoring the use of unreported funds to finance elections. On the other side, the project's critics assert that the secrecy and lack of transparency around the plan will encourage money laundering instead, making the initiative contentious.

The fundamental right of residents and voters to know how a political party is supported will be violated by this. Given that the donor's identity is unknown, there may be an influx of illicit funds. The guarantee of donor "anonymity" imperils democracy itself.

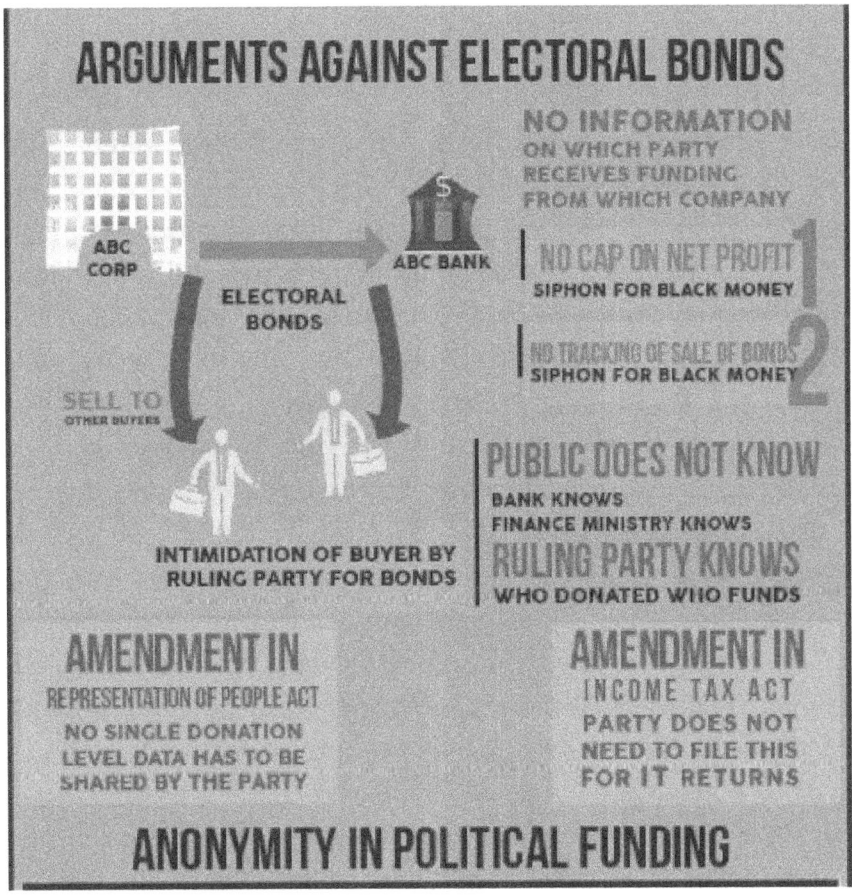

Figure 6: Electoral Bonds
Source: https://www.insightsonindia.com/

Through such bonds, the government can intimidate different enterprises through enforcement agency raids and demand bribes. The government of the day will be aware of who is purchasing the bonds and their value because they are issued through bank accounts that comply with KYC requirements. Today, anyone can donate to political parties anonymously, even international corporations and shell firms. As a result, outside parties or nations may meddle in the administration of sovereign Indian states.

These bonds equate to the institutionalisation of corruption and the legalisation of money laundering. Enforcement officials have frequently and obtrusively raided businesses recently that do not donate through bonds.

Association for Democratic Reforms, a non-profit organisation, filed a public interest lawsuit in 2017 regarding the alleged corruption and subversion of democracy caused by the illegal and foreign funding of political parties and the lack of transparency in the Electoral Bond system. On April 6, 2022, before a bench presided over by Chief Justice N.V. Ramana, advocate Prashant Bhushan—a well-known civil liberties activist and the attorney for the Association for Democratic Reforms (ADR)—reiterated it is a crucial issue that requires an urgent hearing. He cited a news report about a Calcutta-based company that paid Rs forty crore through electoral bonds to ensure no excise raids were conducted on it. No hearing has been held since the court decided to review that matter to see if the current electoral bonds programme promotes anonymous corporate funding of political parties and whether it was incorrectly certified as a Finance Act.

With the introduction of electoral bonds, the BJP's campaign for the 2019 general elections incurred unprecedented amounts of spending and made it excessively opaque and difficult to understand (Jaffrelot, C., & Verniers, G., 2020).

3.4 Media

We live in a highly connected world where we can connect instantly with anyone, anywhere. It has not been so always. Historically, the evolution of media took place seamlessly in waves, transiting from one wave to the next. Jeff Desjardins (Desjardins, J., 2022, July 7) had broadly divided these into three waves after the initial phase of Proto Media (50,000+ years) when the messages were sent across through human activity like oral tradition and manually written text, Wave 1:- Analog and Early Digital Media (1430-2004) when printing press, radio, television and the computer became the norm for communication, Wave Two:-Connected Media (2004-current) when the birth of Web 2.0 and social media prevailed enabling everyone for participation and content creation and reaching the whole world, and Wave 3:-Data Media (2015-current) when an enormous amount of open source data was made available to everyone. With the data of immense proportion, the problem of storage, verification and ascertaining ownership of data cropped. The emerging Web3 blockchain technology may be able to handle this issue.

3.4.1 Social Media

Media has come to be referred to as the Fourth Estate in the 19th century. The origin of the term can best be explained within the context of the medieval estates of the realm. In medieval society, three estates were formally recognised: the clergy, the nobility, and the commoners. Each estate had a very distinct social role and a certain level of power, and the idea of the estates of the realm became entrenched in society. Thus, the media became the fourth estate to enjoy power.

Freedom of the press remained an essential epithet of society, implying the absence of interference from an overreaching state with built-in constitutional and legal safeguards. Everyone has the right to freedom of opinion and expression, including the freedom to hold opinions without interference and impart information and ideas through any media regardless of frontiers, according to the Universal Declaration of Human Rights.

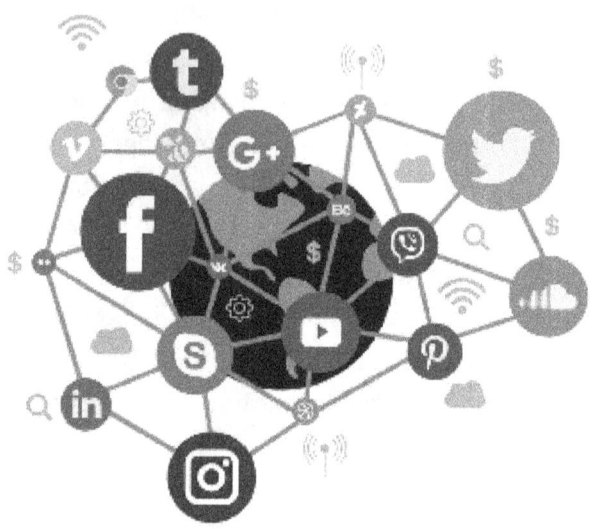

Figure 7: Social Media.

Source: https://cwpwp2.betterthanpaper.com/wp-content/uploads/2019/05/social-media-marketing.png

The traditional media, print as well as TV, has been owned and controlled by vested interests all over the world. The editors and scribes do not have their prerogative to opine or report and often have to toe the strict line of thought set by owners, usually business houses or governments, to suit their interests.

The stronghold of these interests on the media of late has been suffocating and unbearable for the freedom-loving society, and it needed an alternate platform to express itself freely, frankly, without fear, bias or coercion.

This necessitated the conception and birth of social media during the dotcom boom era, and it provided a fertile ground for a plethora of social media platforms like Facebook, Twitter, Linked In, YouTube,

WhatsApp, and the like to mushroom all over merely because of the mere technological advancements in information technology (Figures 7 and 8). China blocked most of the US social media platforms and developed its own set of similar applications like Baidu, WeChat, TikTok, etc. These social media platforms helped billions of people to vent their ire and express themselves freely, causing a death knell to print media.

Governments of all times and hues are known to hold on to information on the pretext of sensitivity by declaring it classified and releasing only filtered information that only works as propaganda and promotes agendas.

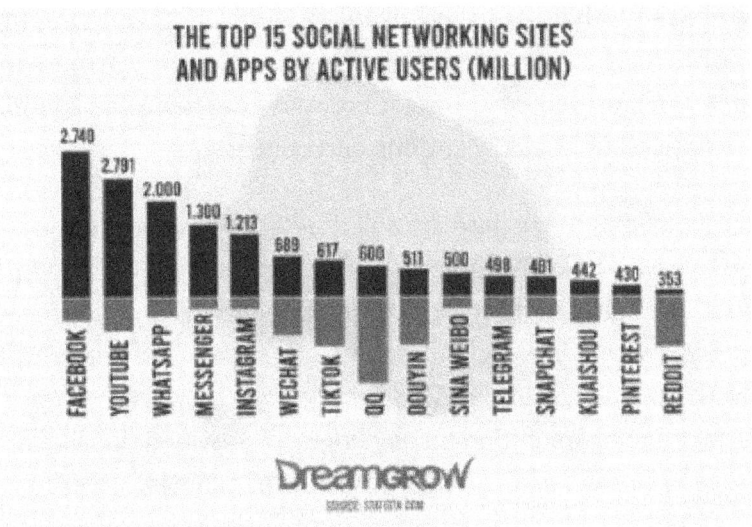

Figure 8: Top 15 Social media sites with active users in millions;
Source: https://www.dreamgrow.com/wp-content/uploads/2021/05/Top-15-Social-Networking-Sites-and-Apps-by-Active-Users-1.webp

Similarly, business houses use the media to promote their products and services without any consideration for the free and fair dissemination of information for the consumption of the unsuspecting public. The media owned by such groups can better be seen merely as an extended advertisement and publicity. The unavailability of information in society leads to corruption so rampant in the Third World or developing countries precisely because of this.

In India, a movement for the right to information started in the early 1990s in Rajasthan, which succeeded in exposing corruption through access to information. It was a triggering point for civil society and led to enacting the Right To Information (RTI) law in many states and the centre in India.

The advent of Social Media has provided a level playing ground to the rich and poor, big or small, equally to put across their viewpoints, vent their frustration, show displeasure at governments and showcase their talent. It has been an uphill task to express your perspective on the day-to-day developments and get your letter to the editor to see the light of day. That is not the case anymore. Anyone can start a blog and start broadcasting their line of thought to get noticed by the contentious and concerned.

Any group of people can have an online video chat, meeting or seminar via Google Meet, Skype, Zoom or similar applications available for free without any cost and form powerful lobby groups and get heard by the powers to be, who do not head to their pleading and lend their ear to the people otherwise. The technology allows even a novice to undertake a sting operation on any unlawful activity or individual. The message or exposure goes viral in a matter of minutes.

Young and new talents can become celebrities overnight by posting their songs, music, and acts on YouTube. They do not need to poach and beg from the recording companies. If your talent is up-to-the-mark, these companies will follow you to sign, thus changing the equation altogether instead of you following them.

The business of the slightest description can reach millions and target audiences without spending millions, thus equalising the equation.

3.4.2 Fake News

Paid and fake news has become the norm of the day these days. Fake news is the byproduct of social media. In this age of social media, facts and the truth is a casualty, and it matters no more (Figure 9). It is the perceptions that matter, and the perceptions are what the propaganda can deliver. It is the deception that is patterned by creating the desired perception. The crux is to invest in propaganda to drive your agenda, however sinister it could be.

Earlier, the modus operandi to hide the facts and truth was the suppression of the data and information. The same objective is achieved by camouflaging the facts with false information, misinformation and propaganda. This is achieved by spreading and fabricating the stories with unverifiable quotes and sources to mislead readers (Desai, S., 2022, May 26). The technological ease of copy-paste and sharing through WhatsApp groups and social media.

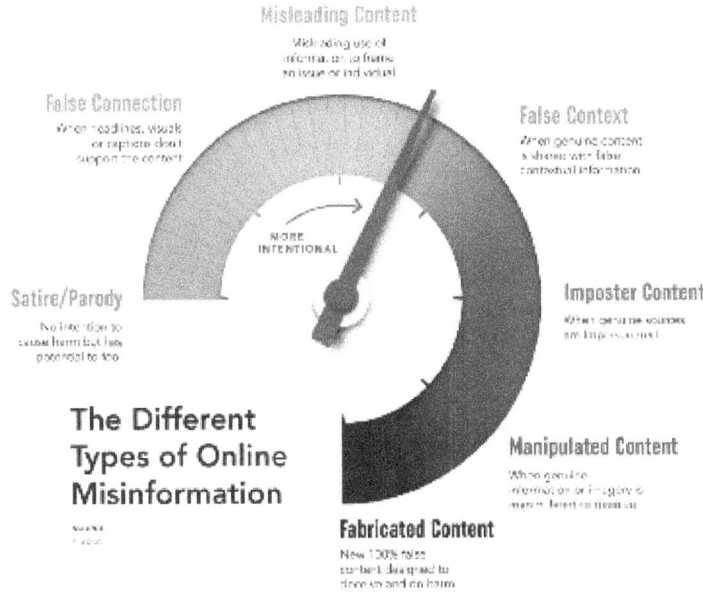

Figure 9: Fake news

Source: https://www.visualcapitalist.com/wp-content/uploads/2021/02/How-to-Spot-Fake-News-full2.jpg

As a result of the increase in fake news, many fact-checking websites and tools have emerged to cross-check and verify the news. The International Fact-Checking Network (IFCN) by Poynter, a nonprofit media institute and newsroom, was launched in 2015 to rally around many individual fact-checkers and fact-checking websites to contain the menace of fake news. For the same purpose, Google has also made a fact-check explorer available at https://toolbox.google.com/factcheck/explorer. Altnews (https://www.altnews.in/), an Indian non-profit fact-checking website founded and run by former software engineers Pratik Sinha and Mohammed Zubairis, is particularly good at busting fake news.

Fake news definitely has economic, political, and social consequences. Its creators, consumers, and arbiters reinforce each other and form a vicious circle that needs to be broken. Fake news comes in two forms, benign misinformation that is simply incorrect and may be inadvertent and disinformation that is deliberate and spread to deceive. This type of disinformation is employed for social engineering and deception purposes that involve a psychological process rather than technological processes to manipulate readers' behaviours (Kshetri, N., & Voas, J, 2017a).

Social media platforms like TikTok, due to fast feedback loops, can train the algorithm and recommend its engines to lead users towards increasingly extreme content, a phenomenon called algorithm radicalisation, a socially undesirable trend (Routley, N., 2022, June 29). Bots are computer-generated algorithms that are easy to create using the application programming interfaces provided by social media platforms. A single user can easily use thousands of such bots. These bots can manipulate discussions and boost certain messages. Such bots are reported to have been used during the 2016 U.S. election (Menczer, F., 2020b, December 1). In 2017 up to 15 per cent of active Twitter users' accounts were bots, and they played a key role in the spread of misinformation, according to a report in Scientific American. Facebook and Twitter influenced the 2020 US elections and the 2019 Indian elections. Social media is believed to have played a vital role and influenced the elections.

Due to the COVID pandemic, more and more people rely on virtual communication. Social media had particularly increased social engagement among first-time tech-savvy millennial voters; however, they got carried away with misinformation, disinformation, fake news, doctored video clips, and memes to engage in political engagement. The 2020 US elections were the most divisive in history. The use and prevalence of artificial intelligence in social media compounded the issue by bombarding the voters with similar content in which they initially showed an interest. The Twitter account of Donald Trump was widely acknowledged and certainly had a tremendous impact on the outcome of the 2016 elections, as he is reported to have had eighty-seven million followers on Twitter at that time.

Data from the Federal Election Commission (Shmargad, Y., & Sanchez, L., 2020) and Twitter metrics of 2016 US congressional election candidates reveal that poorer candidates who spent less than their competitors did better if they had an indirect influence on Twitter by getting their tweets shared by users whose own tweets were widely shared.

Similarly, in India, electronic media has been playing an essential role in Indian elections (Prakash, A., 2019, April 12) since the 2014 elections for public campaigning. Because social media gets advertisements from governments and, as a result, lets them have a free ride for propaganda. As a result, the incumbent party gets an edge over the opposition and can manipulate the media. India is in the top ten countries as far as the number of social media users is concerned. India is understood to have 200 million WhatsApp users, 7.65 million Twitter users, 300 million Facebook users, and forty-one million YouTube users. Apparently, with such a number of social media users, the impact of intensive communications can be decisive.

Social media technologies enable any individual to reach a vast audience simultaneously. This makes it far easier for them to be captured by a limited number of actors. At very little cost, the candidates can bombard the electorate with their political message across the electorate with little accountability and responsibility. Social media like Twitter has helped create and reinforce the personality cult by allowing the creation of a large following through propaganda. This phenomenon was visible in the run-up to the 2019 elections. WhatsApp, in particular, has been responsible for fueling many social conflicts recently, from the persecution of targeted sections of the population to the spread of social unrest and fear through thousands of re-postings and forwards of messages of communally charged veracity of which is rarely an issue.

The social rupture caused by divisive campaigns, including heightened insecurity for marginalised sections of society, was phenomenal. It must be stressed that besides skewing public reasoning, the phenomenon of fake news and misrepresentation through social media has also provided a powerful outlet for undemocratic and unethical evil social forces. Apart from creating social tensions and skewing public reasoning, the density of such transmissions is such that many do not have the ability or wherewithal to distinguish between fact and fiction.

The borderless nature of social media technologies is another dimension of this debate. The non-citizen Indian diaspora played a significant role in influencing the voters and the outcome of the results during the 2014 and 2019 parliamentary elections and 2022 state elections. This trend is likely to continue in the wake of large-scale people migration and the provisions of dual and multinational citizenship. This can be termed as interference without responsibility in the political affairs of other countries in a way. Even the Prime Minister of India, Narendra Modi, while speaking at a diaspora event in the US openly campaigned and chanted slogans in favour of Donald Trump in the 2020 US elections and sought support for himself from the worldwide diaspora. He might be aware that if this support goes in his favour today, it may go against him tomorrow as other party leaders will approach the diaspora. The exercise of public reasoning seems to have taken a backseat, with each side addressing its own echo chamber through social media. Un-anchored social media campaigns had an essential impact on the 2019 elections.

Many sections of society, fearing such electoral skews, have been able to string together alliances with other such actors to contest the political campaigns based on fake news or misrepresentation to bring the political debate back to the basic issues of social cohesion and transformative socio-economic change.

WhatsApp seems to be the source of many and ends up as a vehicle of fake news and misinformation. It is being used as a carrier of circulation of forwards as received information without quoting the source or reference of that information within various closed WhatsApp groups, perpetuating and reinforcing their bias and closed worldview.

Most people do not have the time, inclination, or care to investigate as long as it fits their belief system and simply forward it to other groups to circulate. If it does not fit the belief system, they simply ignore it. As a result, misinformation stays as misinformation, does not add any value but instead confirms their cocooned belief system. As the WhatsApp groups are small and people know each other, no one dares to ask questions for fear of others being annoyed.

Whereas in the case of Facebook, your posts are open to and can be viewed by a large audience, and you stand a chance to be listened to, to listen to counterpoints of others and course correction, provided you are favourably disposed to listen to positive criticism, open-minded and are ready to leave your topic of discussion open-ended for others to take the lead.

3.4.3 Polarisation of Society

Social media has provided a platform for everyone to engage, participate and contribute to the discussion. It should work as an equaliser rather than polarising society. Some social media networks like Twitter tend to be centralised, which allows the leaders and celebrities to create a following to send their messages across a wide public, a sort of one-way traffic, where these small number of people are at the centre of the network and are connected to lots of other people on the periphery. The multitude of people at the periphery has comparatively few connections, while the few at the centre are nearly connected to everyone. The people at the centre may sway and manipulate the people at the periphery, create a personality cult, drive an agenda and misguide the people. The people at the periphery are in a vulnerable situation. If the people at the centre send partisan messages, this can quickly spread like a fire, creating social rupture and discord. In these centralised networks, the ideas are filtered through, planted or sometimes even blocked by powerful resourceful individuals for political or financial gains. Twitter seems to have played a significant role in creating polarisation in society in light of the above argument. In India, rising incidents of identity-based violence are the result of a tacit and overt sanction of majoritarian and populist politics (Mirchandani, M., 2018, August 29). Unlike Twitter, Facebook is an egalitarian platform where everyone can engage and participate in the ongoing debate on an equal footing.

3.4.4 Muzzling the Media

In India, questioning the government has become a penal offence, and its critics have been painted as criminals and anti-Indians since the BJP came to power in 2014. This practice has become a norm rather than an exception. It included painting student leaders like Kanhahaya Kumar as Naxal and anti-Indian. It demonised the farmers protesting against the three farm laws along the border of Delhi and protests against the Citizenship Amendment Act at Shaheen Bagh, Delhi. Sedition charges have been laid against so many, like climate activist Disha Ravi, and the National Security Act has been routinely used against activists, writers, cartoonists and other members of civil society.

An archaic piece of legislation, Section 124A of the Indian Penal Code, enacted by the British in 1870 to suppress the revolt against the empire during the independence of India for the independence of the country, is freely used to suppress dissent in India against anyone who dares to ask questions. Incidentally, this is the same law used by the British to jail Mahatma Gandhi.

3.4.5 Media Monopolies

The media includes news, print and publication, digital, recording, advertising, broadcasting and networking, motion pictures and their associated infrastructure. Media is a main source of information for the public to be better informed to engage in public discourse. The media is one of the four pillars of democracy after the Legislative, Judicial and Executive. Without a balanced and independent media, democracy can not function as a true government of the people, for the people and by the people. The public will remain ignorant and prone to manipulation by a selective and biassed presentation of information in the absence of fair and independent media. It will lead to control of public opinion and pose a threat to free speech and freedom of expression, giving rise to authoritarianism. Independent media is a prerequisite for a functional, healthy democracy.

Nowadays, it is an open secret that media ownership has concentrated in the hands of a few in all the developed democracies across the globe. This concentration of media in the hands of a few is tantamount to the instrumentalisation (Hallin, D., & Mancini,

P., 2004) of media, a term used by Hallin and Mancini (2004) to describe the control of media for an ulterior motive of seeking economic and political benefits. Moreover, it is an antithesis of and contradicts the basic tenets of democracy.

Although there have been many public-spirited and public-interest campaigns by civil societies and activists recently for many important social issues like environmental protection, consumer protection and human rights protection, surprisingly, no such sustained campaign has ever been initiated or organised against the issue of concentration of media in the hands of a few, that can and has lead to abuse of political power. The case of Silvio Berlusconi can be cited as an example, who had a 40 per cent stake in TV media and used a narrative in favour of his political party in 1994 in Italy (Graham, A., & Davies, G., 1997).

Globalisation has further accentuated the problem by facilitating the emergence of cross-media conglomerate transnational ownership like Time Warner/AOL, Pearson and Bertelsmann in the US (Figure 10). The issues of concentration, cross-platform ownership and corporatisation of media have created a nexus between corporations and politicians to the detriment of the citizens.

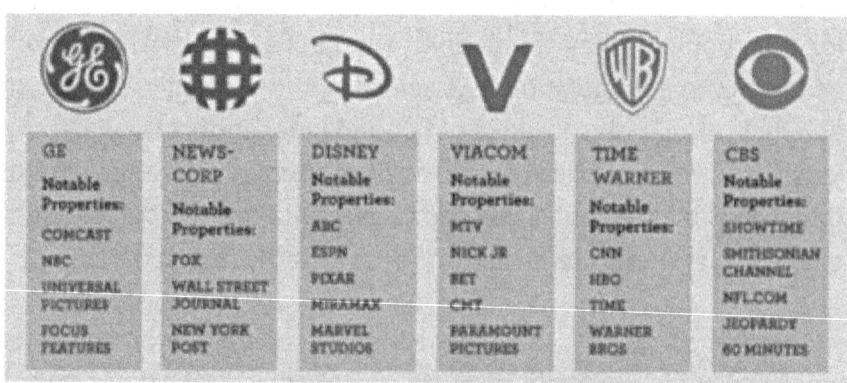

Figure 10: Media ownership US

Source: https://www.thecommonsenseshow.com/siteupload/2016/10/media-ownership.jpg

As monopolies in business ownership pose problems in the economic marketplace, similarly, the concentration of media ownership in the hands of a few poses problems in the marketplace of ideas. The concentration of media ownership in the hands of a few is harmful to the freedom of expression, as it limits the free flow of ideas and information in society, which is detrimental to a healthy democracy. It is a fundamental requirement in a democracy to have a well-informed, inclusive, and pluralistic public sphere. The media has the potential to exert political pressure by influencing the public sphere to the detriment of the democratic value system. These few owners, who are essentially the corporations, having monopolistic control over the media, can exercise excessive control over the politicians and the government to covertly manipulate political decisions and get unique hidden economic benefits. The nexus between the corporate media and the politicians can and has widened the divide between the rich and poor, and the rich will keep getting richer, whereas the poor will keep getting poorer. This can eventually lead to social unrest.

In the US, only six media conglomerates, sometimes referred to as global media oligopoly (Herman, E., & McChesney, R., 1997), viz General Electric, Walt Disney, New Corporation, Time Warner, Viacom and CBS Corporation, are controlling the media. Instead of being the voice of the public as the fourth pillar for a healthy democracy, the media has emerged as a tool in the hands of corporations and politicians to stifle civil and political involvement and create a narrative suiting their own ends. Though, there is antitrust legislation to discourage the concentration of business ownership in the United States designed to boost competition by preventing monopolies and concentrations of business ownership, as well as practices such as price fixing associated with them. But changes to antitrust enforcement were introduced in 1980, claiming that exercising control on the monopolies was an inherently anti-free market and that monopoly prices would better be defeated by the market forces itself rather than antitrust laws (Shen, D., 2012).

In India, the world's biggest media market, the media is controlled by a few powerful people with strong political links (figure 11), according to the Reporters Without Border organisation, which is indicative of a symbiotic relationship between politics and business. The Media Ownership Monitor (MoM) India has 111,239 publications and 880 satellite TV channels (Anon., 2019, June 29). Ambani owns about 70 per cent of the media outlets, including Network 18, and Adani owns a stake in Quint and recently took control of 29% of the stake in NDTV in a hostile takeover.

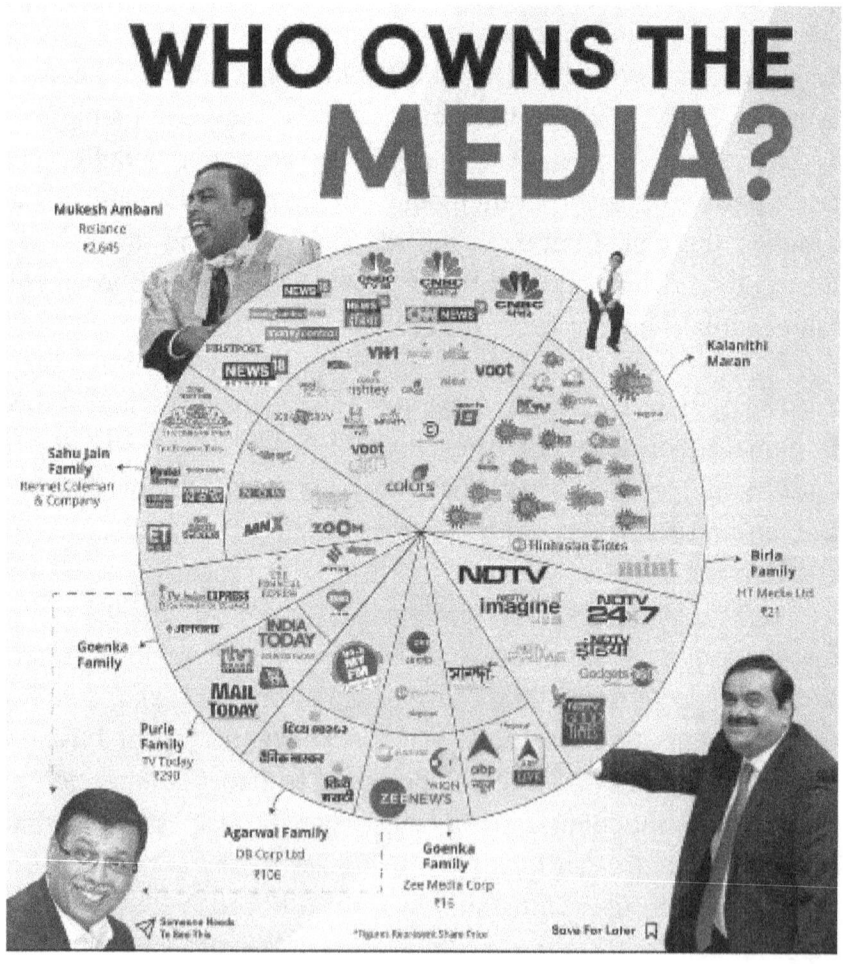

Figure 11: Who owns the media?
Source: https://tinyurl.com/2zpdw64p

Such a stronghold on the media is an attempt to ensure that there is no mass mobilisation to challenge their brute authority over decision-making. Ordinary people tend to think their right to vote gives them the ultimate ticket to power, which is a fallacy.

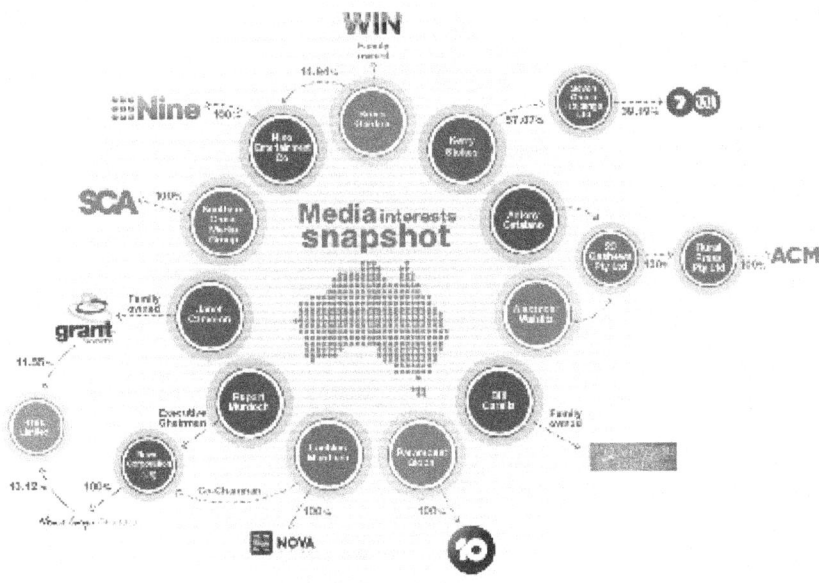

Figure 12: Media Interests snapshot, Australia
Source: https://channelfinder.acma.gov.au/webwr/media-ownership/MediaInterests Snapshot.jpg

In Australia (Figure 12), Media Ownership Regulation prevents the common ownership of newspapers, television and radio broadcasting licences that serve the same region. The purpose of the legislation is to encourage diversity in the ownership of the most effective forms of commercial media: the daily press and free-to-air television and radio. The justification for the rules is that the effective functioning of a democracy requires diverse ownership of the daily mass media to ensure that public life is reported fairly and openly. In Australia, the Australian Competition & Consumer Commission (ACCC) is the apex body that oversees monopolistic tendencies.

The monopoly of media may be at any level - national or international; may be of any nature - commercial or government; of any media outlets such as newspapers, film, television, radio, and satellite broadcasting; or maybe on a national or international level. If the government has a monopoly over media, it may use it for propaganda, restrict freedom of expression, repression of dissent, injustice and exploitation.

Scanning the articles in peer-reviewed journals and analysis of the academic research data (Figures 10, 11 and 12) clearly indicates that the corporations have created and modelled a gigantic web of corporate media empires that caters to and fulfil the desires and needs of these corporations.

3.5 Political Infirmities

3.5.1 Political Correctness

Political correctness is when politicians are reluctant to even talk about the issues, let alone act upon and work on them, for fear that some segments of the public may be offended. When, rather than being an aberration, such behaviours become the norm, it is political correctness. What is the politically correct phenomenon? How and why has this become so pernicious and pervasive, and what are the contributing factors?

Social media is the major contributory factor for developing this behaviour on the part of politicians. This is one of the adverse effects of social media that politicians need to overcome in the long term if they want to stay in the game and be effective. It's likely that the good one will find a way to escape.

Because the media has given everyone a platform and an opportunity to voice their opinions on everything, they do so without pausing to consider the gravity and significance of the situation or the point made; instead, using emotion and prejudice instead of logic, reason and implications.

Instead of being debated, the issue becomes a flash point quickly grabbed by these people, who end up merely as trolls and have no role to play other than ridicule and create noise. Sometimes these gullible trolls get picked up by the mischievous mob with an ulterior motive and at whom the issue is directed, and who are the only ones at the point of attention and eye of the storm. Politicians are diverted from pressing policy issues by political correctness, which keeps them preoccupied with irrelevant, inconsequential, and pointless conversations. Evidently, the threat of political correctness ensnares a lot of politicians. Political correctness keeps lawmakers babbling inane rubbish and stops them from focusing on crucial policy issues.

3.5.2 Opinion Surveys

The second-most popular category, opinion surveys, has significantly contributed to the spread of the political correctness plague, which is rife today.

The perception is that the opinion polls aim to gauge and represent the public's sentiment on the hottest issues of the day. Unfortunately, the politicians seem to take these surveys seriously and mould their behaviour and actions as intended by the promoters and financiers of these surveys.

As a result, instead of focusing on important issues, long-term strategies, and action plans, politicians wind up responding to and modifying themselves to their whims.

Politicians should be aware that the polls' true goal is not to evaluate public opinion but rather to influence it to the liking of the masters running the surveys and pulling the strings behind the scenes, turning them into puppets.

3.5.3 Identity Politics

The term identity politics was initially used by Barbara Smith, a Black feminist, in 1974 (Garza, A., 2019, September 24). Recently, identity politics has been in the limelight and getting a lot of attention, mostly in a negative context (Oliver, T., 2018, June 26). In view of the large-scale population migration facilitated by globalisation, a mixing of cultures and values is taking place. The people find themselves a little bit lost because of a feeling of not being recognised in the surrounding societies after relocating and try to assert their identity by creating pressure groups and seeking political attention. The other social groups based on language, religion, ethnicity, sex and sexual orientation also indulge in the same practice. This type of feeling of lack of not getting the respect that you think you deserve makes you uncomfortable. There are chances of you being driven towards violence and religious fanaticism, creating fragmentation of society and an "Us vs Them" mentality.

When the politicians start playing up, aligning or appeasing these groups for their own advantage to establish their vote bank, they are encouraging identity politics. When politicians start pitching one social group against the other, it acquires a negative tone, causing divisions in society. The idea that people vote based on their identity stereotypes the groups by putting the group in boxes.

The resurgence of identity politics of various groups aided by globalisation is one of the major puzzles of the contemporary political world. Political action groups based on collective identity promotion are evident everywhere these days (Brown, D. L., 2012).

Everyone is, of course, different and should think for themselves. Going with a particular ideology based on our race rather than the ideology we stand for makes us politically ignorant, which is harmful to us and our democracy. As a result, many people end up voting for issues they are actually opposed to and against without even noticing it. There lies the problem for and source of identity conflict.

Identity politics is another issue like political correctness that refers to political positions based on the interests and perspectives of social groups with which they identify. As identity politics deepens the divides between different groups in society, it is destructive and negatively affects the polity.

For example, the Black Lives Matter campaign in the US weaponised identity politics after the killing of a black, George Floyd, by a white policeman, causing a lot of rancour and distrust between white majorities and ethnic minorities (Heffer, S., 2021, August 31). Simon Heffer, a historian from the United Kingdom, argues that the danger of identity politics lies in its ability to turn rational people of the oppressor majority into self-hating irrational people. This behaviour is perpetuated by social media that generally bypasses the rationalistic checks in the debate and rather whips up hostile emotions against those who disagree with them.

3.5.4 Post-Truth and Demagoguery

When objective facts are less influential in shaping public opinion than appeals to emotion and personal beliefs, it becomes post-truth. Post-truth politics is a political culture where the debates get entangled in the true-false narrative, relegating the real issues confronting society to the backseat. When the agreement on the facts gets splintered, the claims become subjective (Enfield, N., 2019), and the world's best thinkers come forward and challenge what is presented to us as fact. Lee McIntyre, a Research Fellow at the Centre for Philosophy and History of Science at Boston University and an Instructor in Ethics at Harvard Extension School, traces the history of developments of the post-truth phenomenon from denial of science, fake news and our psychologically blind spots in his book, Post-Truth (McIntyre, L., 2018c).

for issues they are actually opposed to and against without even noticing it. There lies the problem for and source of identity conflict.

Identity politics is another issue like political correctness that refers to political positions based on the interests and perspectives of social groups with which they identify. As identity politics deepens the divides between different groups in society, it is destructive and negatively affects the polity.

For example, the Black Lives Matter campaign in the US weaponised identity politics after the killing of a black, George Floyd, by a white policeman, causing a lot of rancour and distrust between white majorities and ethnic minorities (Heffer, S., 2021, August 31). Simon Heffer, a historian from the United Kingdom, argues that the danger of identity politics lies in its ability to turn rational people of the oppressor majority into self-hating irrational people. This behaviour is perpetuated by social media that generally bypasses the rationalistic checks in the debate and rather whips up hostile emotions against those who disagree with them.

3.5.4 Post-Truth and Demagoguery

When objective facts are less influential in shaping public opinion than appeals to emotion and personal beliefs, it becomes post-truth. Post-truth politics is a political culture where the debates get entangled in the true-false narrative, relegating the real issues confronting society to the backseat. When the agreement on the facts gets splintered, the claims become subjective (Enfield, N., 2019), and the world's best thinkers come forward and challenge what is presented to us as fact. Lee McIntyre, a Research Fellow at the Centre for Philosophy and History of Science at Boston University and an Instructor in Ethics at Harvard Extension School, traces the history of developments of the post-truth phenomenon from denial of science, fake news and our psychologically blind spots in his book, Post-Truth (McIntyre, L., 2018c).

> *"We have some of the best minds from everywhere; law, politics, philosophy, media, science, medicine – all wrestling with how we can protect the integrity of the information that all those disciplines are built on,"* – Professor Nick Enfield.

The political culture is where a narrative is formed by cloaking the policy details by appealing to emotions and rebutting and ignoring the facts on purpose to mislead by deception. This is achieved through disinformation, falsification and negating expert opinion. It can be ascertained by the enlightened by looking at the leaders if they are walking the talk or taking you for granted and avoiding pertinent questions. This methodology is usually adopted for their ulterior motives by right-wing extremists and jihadis equally (Köhler, D., & Ebner, J., 2019). There is a recent rise of post-truth demagoguery and right-wing authoritarianism, causing extensive damage to the free press and de-legitimation of science.

According to Sebastian Vattamattam (Vattamattam, S., 2020, February 21), in the aftermath of the September 11, 2001 attack on the Twin Towers when the US, in its efforts to retaliate, started fabricating political lies that ushered the post-truth era in the west. The US invaded Iraq on the pretext of suspected weapons of mass destruction. It reached its zenith with the presidential elections in 2016 when Donald Trump came to power. Fascist regimes in the past have used such rhetoric in the past. The frequently and regularly repeated political lies make people at large indifferent to truth, and having lost the sense of truth, they lose their sense to criticise power, thereby making the governments autocratic and fascist. Fascism is a sociopolitical phenomenon that excludes certain inhabitants based on race, religion or ethnicity from its new definition of a nation. The US introduced the Immigration Act of 1924 to prevent immigration from Asian countries. Hitler ostracised Jews and passed Nuremberg laws in 1935, drawing inspiration from the US. Recently, the BJP government in India passed the Citizenship

(Amendment) Act 2019 to prevent the immigration of Muslims from neighbouring countries.

In the 2014 Indian general elections, Narendra Modi came to power by creating a false sense among voters to regain some elusive glorious past, causing disenchantment and anger against the Muslim minorities and holding them responsible for the excesses perpetrated by their predecessors, the Mughal Emperors. In the 2016 US election, Donald Trump used this technique to awaken bigotry, arouse hate and normalise deception (Gross, M., 2017).

Pankaj Mishra, an Indian writer and author of the book Age of Anger: A History of the Present, argues that because of the failure of Enlightenment rationalism to account for the emotional needs of the people has led to the rise of such anti-intellectual authoritarian leaders. This has been aided further by people's indifference to this emotional need and recent economic sufferings caused by modern capitalism. The false and misplaced assumption that there is no alternative to western-style capitalism and failure to visualise the emerging trends shaping the new world order has added fuel to the fire. Most existing English literature has been written from the US and Western perspectives.

3.6 Self-Immolation of Democracy - Right-Wing Extremism

About twenty years after the September 11, 2001 attack, commonly known as the 9/11 attack, on the Twin Towers of the World Trade Centre and Pentagon in New York, US, and the ensuing offensives dubbed as the global war on terror by the US the world is now confronting a new threat from far-right extremism (Ashby, H., 2021, January 15). The ideas and groups from far-right extremism, from Brazil, the US, and Hungary to New Zealand and India, pose a grave danger to the democratic value system and societies. According to Jacinda Arden, Prime Minister of New Zealand, the ideas and language of hate already existed in society for many decades, but their form of dissemination and tools of the organisation has changed. In 2019, the deadly attack in Christchurch, New Zealand, underscored this phenomenon. Social media and WhatsApp groups have facilitated its spread across borders.

Right-wing extremism is taking place in both economically developed liberal democracies like the US, Norway, Germany, Italy, and New Zealand etc. and also developing democracies like Brazil and India (Campion, K., & Poynting, S., 2021). In India, BJP, a right-wing party headed by Narendra Modi, came into power in the 2014 elections. Modi has encouraged the extreme factions of his party and normalised the right-wing extremism in the mainstream, playing the Hindu victimhood card and introducing the Citizenship Amendment Bill 2019 that singles out Muslims from the list of persecuted religious groups from the neighbouring countries to be eligible for citizenship. Before becoming the Prime Minister of India, Modi was denied a visa to the US because of his tacit support for and indifference to the attacks on Muslims by Hindu extremist mobs in Gujarat in 2002, when he was the Chief Minister of that state.

Another example of right-wing fanaticism is when on January 6, 2021, thousands of Trump supporters invaded and seized the Capitol Complex in Washington DC extorted by Trump, refusing to accept defeat and calling it a stolen election in defiance of election results. Several hundred far-right extremists attempted to storm the Bundestag Building in Berlin, Germany, in August 2020 against coronavirus restrictions. According to Carter, 2018 profound distrust of democracy is at the heart of far-right extremists (Carter, E., 2018). Far-right extremism is characterised by its hostility towards science and experts, fuelled by its self-perpetuating, self-referencing feedback loops and algorithm bubbles created by social media.

A number of key factors for framing ideological narratives used by far-right extremists can be broadly identified and enumerated as Islamophobia, populism, ethnocentrism, xenophobia, ethno-pluralism, institutional elitism, anti-elitism, nationalism, and law-and-order win elections according to several researchers (Guibernau, M. 2010); (Harrison, S., & Bruter, M., 2011); (Ignazi, P., 1992); (Mudde, C., 2002).

In Australia, the two distinct but connected threats by the rise of anti-democratic right-wing extremism could be identified (Waldek, L., & Droogan, J., 2021, August 16). The first one is shifting the political and social parameters of acceptance to a level that challenges our acceptance of a diverse and functioning multicultural society. The second being of a real-world violent terrorist attack along the lines of what happened in Christchurch, New Zealand. Right-wing extremists are routinely on the lookout for opportunities to appropriate conservative political rhetoric and beliefs to legitimise their radical agenda. Australian security agencies are well aware of the situation. They are applying a three-prong approach to educating and teaching the meaning of democratic values through the formal education system. Applying early intervention strategies to identify and divert people's attention away from violent and divisive political movements, and finally being well aware that the wider corrosive threat to liberal democracy may actually be routed through legal means.

4 Incapacitation of Capitalism

4.1 Background

Society continuously keeps evolving depending on the economic relations between different classes and their political characteristics at that particular time. It evolved over time from the initial primitive communes society (Anon., 2013, February 17) with meagre resources where all members of relatively small tribes used to cooperate to survive with no private property. The advent and emergence of agriculture involving land and cattle brought in the concept of ownership of private property.

Agriculture supported large populations and led to the division of society into haves and have-nots, the enslavers and enslaved people, leading to the slave society. Slavery evolved in parallel with the concept of property ownership. People without property worked as slaves for those who owned land and cattle on their properties. All the resources of survival like land, water and tools to work on them and the workers themselves got under the control of a ruling upper class. In contrast, the workers themselves were left with minimum survival sustenance. The slave empires eventually expanded and became too wealthy and costly to maintain and sustain themselves.

With the accumulation of wealth over and above what was needed in societies, in Rome and other places of significantly advanced areas, a few wealthy people established aristocratic rights over specific areas and regions that evolved into a feudal society. These property rights got carried over from generation to generation based on inheritance, depriving others of such rights to any resource or property. The workers were tied to the land, a landowner in exchange for a portion of the product to be retained by them for subsistence. The emergence of tools, technology and skills dealt the death knell to feudal society. The feudal system devolved into the current system of capitalism during the middle of the 17th century.

As feudalism began to break down, peasants who were forced to work on the lands of their lords as a feudal obligation were gradually replaced by a market-based system of employment: for salary, rent and other allowances. By the middle of the 18th century, the restrictions that prevented the common person from owning property and capital goods were extended equally to all for the first time, and the right to own the means of property and production was gradually removed.

The nobles of the Middle Ages led a luxurious existence and shunned commerce, craft, and commercial enslavement as menial labour. They were more interested in politics, warfare, and pleasure. They inspired envy among those in lower social strata, who therefore started businesses and engaged in commercial endeavours to make money and accumulate wealth. The middle class's drive for a better living set the groundwork for entrepreneurship and the growth of capitalism (Pejovich, S., 1990, January 1). Over time, many ills cropped up in capitalism, too. A discussion about these ills of the current economic system of capitalism has been going on in the western world for a long time (Hanton, A., 2012, January 16). As a result, an anti-capitalist movement has been gaining momentum. However, as the free media is owned by the wealthy, the anti-capitalist side of the debate has remained subdued as it has not been fairly covered.

4 Incapacitation of Capitalism

The common capitalist premise that 'anyone can be rich by working hard and smart enough' is a fallacy because you need money to make money that you have to take from someone else. This means that the rich cannot exist without the poor; therefore, inequality takes place because of the profit motive behind capitalism rather than altruism. In a capitalist democracy, even though every person has a vote, they have very little influence over the government's decisions. The wealthy have a greater influence and say on government in formulating policies than ideology or public opinion. Naturally, the governments will listen to big businesses and banks because they are the ones who fund their election campaigns. Similarly, the governments will listen to newspaper barons because they know they have the capacity to influence public opinion through the media.

Given that capitalism's fundamental and exclusive motivation is profit, it is obvious that most recent conflicts have been excessively profitable with geopolitical consequences to control natural resources, particularly oil. The Iraq war was largely funded by oil barons, and these firms were given contracts for the reconstruction of the country after the devastation and demolition of the infrastructure in Iraq after the initial invasion (Sommerlad, N., 2013, March 23). In Libya, the western forces intervened only when the civil war caused oil supplies to be cut off and sided with the rebels because they thought they were the most likely to win. Similarly, military intervention took place in Iran when the trading routes to transport oil were blocked. The excessive emphasis on earning profit at any cost has diverted capitalism from what it was originally conceptualised.

4.2 What is Capitalism?

Capitalism, by definition, means that individuals have freedom and equal rights to own, manage, and dispose of their capital goods and property as they deem fit for themselves. The origins of capitalism as an ideology can be traced back to the middle of the 17th century when the European economies were predominantly farming and trading. According to Garikai Chengu, capitalism is cancer, as it is based on and works on the principle of growth for the sake of growth, as cancer does. Turning nature into commodities and the commodities into capital is the fundamental tenet of capitalism46. We have reached a point where capitalism is very different from the ideal state of operation theoretically envisioned.

Now, though individuals have equal competitive rights to own the means of production, it is practically impossible for the average individual to compete with corporations that have grown mighty in power and size, practically taking over and replacing the feudal lords of the 1600s and the trusts of the early 1900s. The wealth, commodities, capital, and means of production have accumulated in the hands of a few industrialists managing the corporations. The workers are left to fend for themselves but can choose to work for someone else or themselves.

The accumulation of wealth and the means of production is owned by a smaller and smaller group of people. Their greed and squabbling are hindering social progress, and it has created a large gap in income between the haves and have-nots, leading to internal conflicts that have led to the emergence of the next phase of economic development. It has come to a point where capitalism's limitations and internal contradictions continue to fester, bringing about its inevitable demise and irrelevance.

This has happened because the corporations have been granted and have been able to obtain significant advantages over individuals as regards taxation because the corporations, due to their sheer size and resources, have greater power to negotiate with the governments at the local, state, and federal levels than an individual can even dream. Moreover, corporations develop close relationships with legislators and regulators by funding their electoral campaigns and are in a position to extract help from them regarding crafting favourable legislation to their advantage (Schelling, C., 2019, May 21). They have limited liability against individuals, which reduces their risk of acting in undesirable ways. Corporations often also have advantaged rights to intellectual property ownership and the individual employees who create that capital do not.

The First World War marked the end of the ascendant phase of the capitalist mode of production, which began in the sixteenth century and reached its zenith at the end of the nineteenth century (Anon., 1992, May 1). In his book, "Postcapitalism: A Guide to the Future", Paul Mason has detailed the paradigm of capitalism arising from rapid information technology developments and the failings of the current economic system. Similarly, David Schweickart also presented his case of the collapse of the capitalist system and suggested an alternate and viable system that he called native economic democracy.

Two observations can be safely made from the developments that took place in the last century, (a) The extreme socialism represented by the Soviet empire is not workable anymore, and it collapsed with the disintegration of the USSR. (b) The current capitalistic system has reached a point of no return and has become fully faulty and dysfunctional and is cracking all over as the downfall and decline of the US hegemony are writ large on the wall. The occurrence of successive recessions and some major recessions every ten to fifteen years, like the recessions of 1873 and 1929, is indicative of the failure of capitalism to cope with time. Billions of dollars had to be spent to rescue the governments, and thousands lost their savings, homes, jobs and means of livelihood in 2008.

The discussion about the failure of the capitalistic system and its criticism has been brewing in a hushed tone for a long time in western countries, but the word has not been allowed to spread by the capitalist-controlled media.

Capitalism, being central to the process of globalisation, has been going through a profound restructuring since the 1970s. The internationalisation of capital and the global integration of national economies led to the formation of a transnational capitalist class (Robinson, W. I., & Harris, J., 2000) of elites through transnational corporations. This class comprises transnational corporations and financial institutions like World Bank and IMF that manage and control transnational economic policies, political policies, and media through media conglomeration. The massive loaning programs run by these financial institutions at times compromise the basic lending principles has led to increased incidences of default that scupper the foundations of capitalism.

4.2.1 Non-Performing Assets (NPA) - the Cancer of Capitalism

Non-Performance Assets refer to loans and advances in the banks' books where no principal or interest repayment is received for ninety days in a row. The banks classify the NPAs into four categories, viz. Standard Assets that have been outstanding for 12 months or less with normal risk; Sub Standard Assets when the loans remain outstanding for more than twelve months, and the creditworthiness of the borrower is weak; Doubtful Debts outstanding for over eighteen months fall under this category, the banks are doubtful of their recovery, and Loss Assets when the recovery seems impossible.

How can a debt (Non-Performing Asset), a bad loan, be an asset instead of a liability? To whom are these debts owed? The corporations? Then how the needle of suspicion is pointed, and is the discussion centred around banks instead of corporations? Why should corporations not be under the lens instead of the banks to put the narrative from the proper perspective? Can these corporations be so ruthless and afford to indulge in such a luxury of not only getting away with cash and holding the banks as culprits and getting the narrative turned around its tail without the connivance of the governments? Is it hard to see that some of the money is being passed out to politicians as a bribe for political campaigns for elections?

It is the corporations that are benefitting from this NPA game plan, or the game plan is designed on purpose to benefit the corporations in connivance with politicians. That is precisely the reason corporations are getting more powerful than governments. In such a system, it is the democracies that are being rendered weak, meek and relegated and put on the back foot.

It is a standard practice and a generally accepted point of law that the needle of suspicion always points to that person, party or entity that stands to gain from that particular illegal act or crime. Applying the same principle while analysing the issue of NPAs, it is the corporations who stand to gain, and it is they that should be held accountable for and investigated, not the banks, as is the case now. The reason why it is not happening is that the governments of the day are hand in glove and in the thick of the imbroglio for their immediate gains. The governments and politicians keep changing and moving on every couple of years, while the same corporations stay there and get more powerful every term and every election cycle.

The main motive of corporations is wholly and solely to make a profit. If the governments are being held hostage by the corporations as they fund their elections, how can you imagine the governments working for the citizens? Corporations are always on the lookout for opportunities that create uncertainties in society, like catastrophes, calamities, and epidemics like COVID-19, for them to strike when the public gaze and attention are caught up somewhere else for their survival and to organise food on the table. While millions of people died, lost houses, and lost jobs, the wealth of the corporations had quantum jumps during the COVID-19 pandemic (Figures 13 & 14).

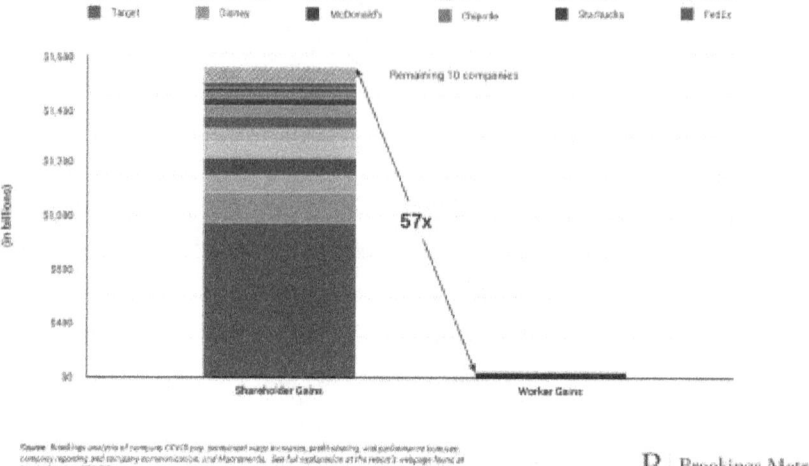

Figure 13: Shareholders of 22 companies grew $1.5 trillion richer, while workers got less than two per cent of the benefit;

Source: https://i0.wp.com/www.brookings.edu/wp-content/uploads/2022/04/Pandemic-Figure-2-1.png?w=768&crop=0%2C0px%2C100%2C9999px&ssl=1

According to an OXFAM report, 'Power, Profit and the Pandemic- From corporate extraction for the few to an economy that works for all', the Global Fortune 500 firms increased their profits by 156%, from USD 820 billion in 2009 to USD 2.1 trillion in 2019. Thirty-two companies from among the world's most profitable companies are expected to make USD 109 billion more during the pandemic than the average of four previous years. Twenty-five individual billionaires increased their worth by a staggering USD 255 billion between mid-March to late May. 2020.

An impression is given, and perception is tried to be created by the corporate lobby that the corporations contribute through tax, philanthropy and social responsibility. The same report clearly bursts this myth: according to this report, the US government lost around $135 billion in revenue due to corporate tax avoidance in 2017, in contrast to their annual philanthropy of less than $ twenty billion. By the same yardstick, the 46 billion in corporate social responsibility in India as compared to the loss of forty-seven billion in government revenue due to corporate tax avoidance annual figure. The corporates are sometimes given a free run as they are seen as the major contributors to the growth of economies.

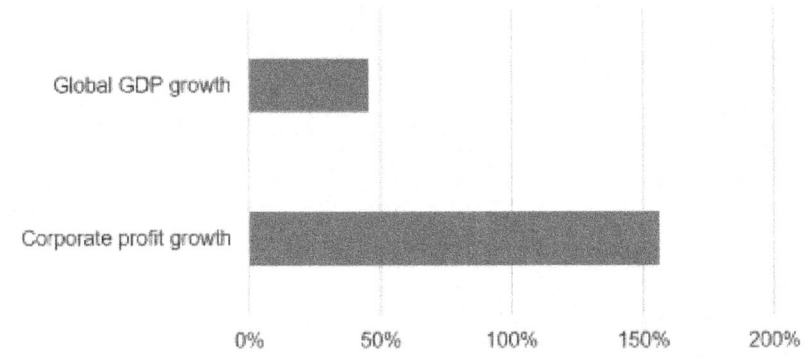

Figure 14: Global Fortune 500 growth vs global GDP growth 2009-19;

Source: Calculations based on Global Fortune 500 data, https://fortune.com/global500/ and World Bank Data, https://worldbank.com/indicator/NY.GDP.MKTP.CD?end=2018start=2009

4.2.2 Gross Domestic Product (GDP) - Growth For the Sake of Growth is a Contagion

GDP is a tool to measure the health of capitalist economies, growth for the sake of growth is a contagion called capitalism. But when you look at how it works and how it is calculated, you would realise it works like chasing your tail and looking for the never-ending pursuit of seeking growth just for the sake of growth. In simple terms, it is like malignancy, killing and demolishing everything along the way, and it keeps multiplying and growing. GDP is an invitation to participate in a race to grow rich and make a profit. The wealth in society is limited. You can grow rich at the cost of somebody else getting poor, thereby amplifying the divide between a few getting rich and the rest getting poor. This has been made clear in the recent pandemic when people lost jobs and houses en masse while a few billionaires enmassed their wealth. This division ultimately leads to social unrest and civil riots, as evidenced and documented in history at length.

The Gross Domestic Product (GDP) is measured by adding up consumer expenditure (C) + Business Investments (I) + Government spending (G) + Net exports X (Exports - Imports) (Figure 15). It is used to measure the economy's health and is considered an indicator of prosperity in an economy. Indirectly, it is a measure of money made by the interaction of production and consumption in the economy. To keep the economy in good health, you need to produce more, consume more and spend more. In other words, growth is for the sake of growth instead of finding a sustainable balance, knowing fully well that our resources are not unlimited. It is generally believed that growth for the sake of growth is a driving force behind capitalism.

> *"Growth is a core tenet of success. But we often destroy our greatest innovations by the constant pursuit of growth. An idea emerges, takes hold, crosses the chasm, hits a tipping point, and starts a meteoric rise with seemingly limitless potential. But more often than not, it implodes, destroying itself in the process. Ideas are consumed just like lichen. Rather than endless growth, the goal should be to grow as quickly as possible — what technologists call hypergrowth — until the breakpoint is reached. Then stop and reap the benefits of scale alongside stability. What is missing — what everyone is missing — is that the unit of measure for progress isn't size; it's time."*
>
> — Jeff Stibel

Growth for the sake of growth has probably reached its zenith and marked the start of the downfall of capitalism. Climate change concerns and the issues and problems that surround it result from the continued harm that consumerism and unrelenting growth are doing to the environment.

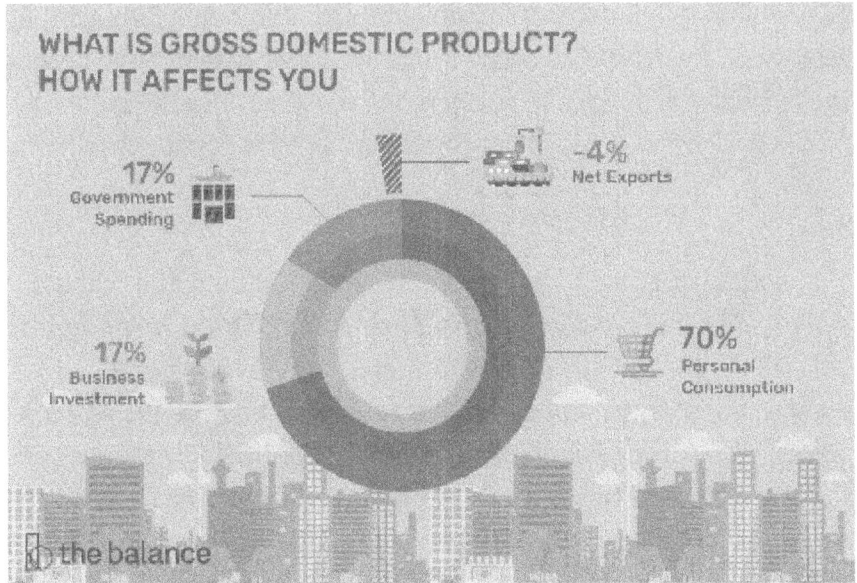

Figure 15: What is Gross Domestic Product, and how does it affect you?
Source: https://www.thebalance.com/what-is-gdp-definition-of-gross-domestic-product-3306038

The GDP is seen as the only barometer to measure the success of business in capitalist economies. By focusing only on money, we are ignoring human-centric factors.

> *"Growth for the sake of growth is the ideology of the cancer cell."*
>
> – Edward Abbey, a writer and environmental activist

In Bhutan, a tiny country tucked in the lap of the Himalayas, nations' success is gauged differently. In 1972 King Jigme Singye Wangchuck declared that the Gross National Happiness is more important than GDP and coined the term Gross Happiness Index and followed sustainable development rather than going for unabated consumerism and endangering the environment. The Gross Happiness Index or the Gross National Happiness is measured by conducting a yearly survey and recording the following nine factors: Psychological well-being, Health, Education, Time Use, Cultural diversity and resilience, Good governance, Community vitality and Ecological diversity resilience. Ironically, what is largely valued by the current version of capitalism is not these positive indicators but rather the opportunities that emerge as a result of catastrophes.

4.2.3 Shock Doctrine

The shock doctrine's fundamental tenet is that the capitalist markets use moments of tragedy or calamity to propose or impose policies that are advantageous to them. This method benefits from people's inability to respond at these moments. A Canadian social activist and author, Naomi Klein (Klein, N., 2014), in her book, 'The Shock Doctrine, The Rise of Disaster Capitalism, argues that the neoliberal free-market policies based on the economic policies of Milton Friedman were deliberately introduced in some countries as a strategy known as shock therapy at the behest of corporations.

A complex system of disaster capitalism involves a series of networks and influences employed by private companies to profit from the disaster, like looking for opportunities in adversity. The invasion of Iraq was a comprehensive and full-scale implementation of shock doctrine to shock and awe, leading to the mass privatisation of Iraq's state-owned enterprises.

These policies veer around the exploitation of natural calamities or political upheavals and thrust questionable and controversial practices while the citizens are emotionally and physically exhausted and distracted and are not in a position to resist. A recent case of introducing the agriculture laws passed by the Narendra Modi government at the peak of the COVID-19 epidemic can be cited as an example of a purportedly handing over agriculture to his crony capitalist friends. The laws, however, had to be rescinded due to unprecedented and prolonged protests by farmers that lasted for 268 days, and 370 farmers died during the course of the agitation (Sandhar, H., 2022). Naomi Klein further argues that the Iraq war was entrusted with pushing through such an agenda. The war would eventually prop up the share prices of the oil companies in the stock markets, which are always on the lookout for these triggers.

4.2.4 Stock Market

A stock market is a marketplace where investors buy and sell company shares. It is a place where companies issue shares and other securities for trading. A stock market index (Figure 16) is a hypothetical portfolio of investment holdings representing a financial market segment. The index is calculated from the prices of the underlying stock holdings. The variation of various stock market indexes is a gauge of the market. The most popular stock market indexes are the Dow Jones Industrial Average (DJIA), S&P 500 Index, Nasdaq Composite Index, FTSE All-World Index, ASX All Ordinaries, Nikkei 225, BSE Sensex, Shanghai SE A Share, etc.

The stock market works through a network of exchanges like NASDAQ, the New York Stock Exchange, etc., where the companies list their shares through a process called an Initial Public Offering (IPO) to raise money to grow their business. The buyers buy shares by offering a bid on the asking price for trading. The price settings offered and bids are calculated through computerised programs involving complex algorithms. The concept of shareholders and having an ownership stake has disappeared because of the web of corporate governance designed to defraud genuine shareholders and avoid paying taxes.

A "share" is the interest of a shareholder in the company measured by a sum of money; for liability in the first place and the interest in the second, but also consisting of a series of mutual covenants entered by all the shareholders following the company's act. In simple terms, a "share" is a bundle of rights and responsibilities given to a shareholder given to him/her in exchange for an investment.

Figure 16: Stock Market Index;

Source: https://i.guim.co.uk/img/media/c17393f18aefefe55a9f7456e096f8a03354314a/0_285_7411_4447/master/7411.jpg?width=620&quality=85&auto=format&fit=max&s=d5f5e86e13e16c58218fd1d971d217d1

A share is like property; the property has an owner and can be bought, sold, gifted, or transferred. In return for investing in a company, a shareholder gets rights within the company, which may vary according to the type of share acquired and are subject to the company's articles of association. Most companies have only one class of shares, i.e., ordinary shares. Though companies can create different classes of shares depending on what sort of shareholder rights they want to assign to them, like founders, investors, and even employees of the company.

Three key rights attached to shares are voting, profit-sharing, and liquidation rights. Usually, ordinary shares carry one vote at general meetings, but there may be non-voting shares or shares with multiple votes as determined by the company's articles. Dividends are payments made on each share of stock that are used to distribute the company's profits.

The company's Articles of Association can divide the company's shares into different classes and allow the directors (or shareholders) to allocate different amounts of dividends to other classes of shares. In the event that the company is liquidated, after paying all the creditors, the remaining assets are available for division among the shareholders. Generally, residual assets are divided among the members in proportion to their respective interests in the company's share capital. If the shares are divided into different classes, the company's Articles may provide for some shares to be given priority in the distribution of the residual assets.

When the company grows in size and operations, it may have to issue shares in different classes to accommodate the interests of its growing number of stakeholders. Ordinary shares are the most common class of shares that carry one vote per share, receive equal dividends, and distribute residual assets among themselves after all the debts have been paid in case the company is liquidated.

These shares are issued to employees to pay their remuneration as dividends as a part of the tax planning strategy for the company and the employee. Members of the principal shareholders' families can also get non-voting shares.

Redeemable Shares are shares the company is bound to buy back or redeem, in other words, at some future date. The date may be fixed or set at the directors' discretion. These shares have no voting rights and are suitable and meant for employees who can encash them when they leave the company, even otherwise.

Generally, Preference Shares carry no voting rights but guarantee dividends, either cumulative, allowing holders to receive payments before ordinary shareholders or non-cumulative, which do not carry rights to claim dividends in case the company has a problem.

On the other hand, management shares carry additional voting rights for promoters to retain control over the company. This may be done by conferring multiple votes to each share or by having a smaller nominal value for such shares so that there are more shares for every dollar invested. A dual-class share is meant to differentiate and delink voting rights from profit-sharing rights and give founders and management an upper hand over ordinary shareholders. Thus many shareholders are simply given a false sense of ownership.

4.2.5 Delusion of shareholders

You may be tempted to think or under the illusion that the shareholders of a corporation own the corporation. The question of who owns the corporation is controversial because of the two versions of capitalism. One side has the protection of shareholders as its core value at its heart, while the other prefers other stakeholders like employees, customers, and the general community in which it operates. According to Peter Georgescu (Georgescu, P., 2021, July 21), looking after only the shareholders has proved catastrophic for the American people and has rendered American corporations incompetent against the economic policies of China. This form of shareholders-centric capitalism is devoid of ethics and morals, with its singular motive of profit only. According to this type of American capitalism, the majority of value creation goes to the Chinese government. This observation of Peter Georgescu prompts me to conclude two things. The first inference is that Chinese capitalism prioritises the interests of the community. The second and most important inference is that the Chinese government transformed itself into a corporation, precluding any private individual from taking over the government and thus acting like a "State" corporation.

Shareholders-centric corporate governance prefers shareholders as primary stakeholders and focuses on maximising the value of shareholders over society in general, community, employees and consumers. This type of corporate governance is called shareholder primacy.

A number of companies allocate ownership rights to stakeholders different from shareholders, despite the fact that the law attributes these rights to the equity holders (Zattoni, A., 2011).

4.3 Behind the Corporate Veil

"Behind the corporate veil" refers to the actions and activities that occur within a corporation but are hidden from public view or oversight because of the legal concept of the corporate veil. The corporate veil is a legal principle that separates the legal identity of a corporation from its shareholders, officers, and directors, shielding them from personal liability for the actions of the corporation. This means that the shareholders, officers, and directors are protected from being held personally liable for any debts or legal judgments against the corporation as long as they have not engaged in fraudulent or illegal activities.

However, the concept of piercing the corporate veil can be applied by courts when the separate legal identity of the corporation is being used to commit fraud or evade legal responsibilities, allowing the individuals behind the corporate veil to be held liable for the corporation's actions.

In general, the corporate veil is used to protect shareholders, officers, and directors from personal liability, but it can also be used to conceal illegal or unethical activities within the corporation.

> *"Almost every economic crime involves the misuse of corporate entitie-money launderers exploit cash-based businesses and other legal vehicles to disguise the source of their illicit gains, bribe-givers and recipients conduct their illicit transactions through bank accounts opened under the*

names of corporations and foundations, and individuals hide or shield their wealth from tax authorities and other creditors through trusts and partnerships to name but a few examples. In recent years the issue of the misuse of corporate entities for illicit purposes has drawn increasing attention,"
— Donald J Johnston, Secretary-General of OECD.

4.3.1 Shell Companies

A shell company is a type of company that exists only on paper and does not have any significant operations or assets. It is often used as a veil to hide the identity of the true owners or to facilitate illegal activities.

Shell companies are usually private companies, limited liability companies or trusts. They don't really exist physically other than having just a postal address, generating no income, and practically no economic value. Though shell companies may exist only on paper, they have a real and deleterious effect on the world. These are used by criminals for financial crimes like contraband sale, selling illegal drugs, hostile takeovers, real estate, holding intellectual property rights, income tax evasion, creating black money and money laundering by creating overinflated and false invoices, fictitious consultancy fees and bogus loans.

Criminal activities are undertaken by concealing the identities of the owners and business activities by obscuring company structures, ownership and activities. In the recent past, we have witnessed numerous such scandals that have been occasionally leaked through reports like Wikileaks, Panama Papers, Paradise Papers and Swiss Leaks exposing such criminal malpractices.

It is an irony that shell companies are legal in almost all countries of the world despite the knowledge of them being apparently and grossly used for such dangerous activities. In the US, the Securities and Exchange Commission permits the use of shell companies as part of a manoeuvre called reverse merger that lets businesses go public without an initial public offering (IPO) (Anon., 2021, November 18). Shell companies are usually located in Switzerland, Bermuda, Seychelles, or the Cayman Islands; the well-known tax havens (figure 17) are designed to cater exclusively to these services and form the major chunk of the economies of these island nations.

Now you may wonder why these shell companies are not while it is easy, and we have more than enough reasons to do so because the company's jurisdiction has lenient tax laws, the creator of the company never has to reveal themselves, and they always use a nominee director and have their lawyer or accountant provide verification. It is hard to identify them unless there is suspicious activity.

4.3.2 Money Laundering

To conceal true ownership, corporations indulge in money laundering as a corporate veil. Money laundering involves hiding the source of money obtained through criminal and illegal means. Usually, it involves three steps, graphically represented in the following diagram (Figure 18): placement (moving the funds to remove their connection with the crime), layering (disguising the trail of money) and integration (bringing the money back to seemingly legitimate activities and sources. The underlying activities that give rise to the need for money laundering include drug, arms, human trafficking, extortion, bribery, insider trading, credit card frauds, illicit tax practices like profit skimming, double invoicing, and diversion of income etc.

New World Order: The Rise of Transnational Corporate Republic

Figure 17: The World's biggest tax havens
Source: https://www.visualcapitalist.com/worlds-biggest-private-tax-havens/

As stated by Donald J Johnston, Secretary-General of OECD, almost every economic crime involves the misuse of corporate entities. The needle of suspicion definitely points towards corporations. These corporate entities operate from countries that create an environment for such activities and provide tight secrecy about the entities. Shell company structure through partnerships, trusts, and foundations is the modus operandi of such operators. The countries that provide such services are referred to as tax havens. Bearer shares, nominee shareholders, nominee directors, flea causes, and letters of wishes are the instruments usually made available to obscure the identity of the beneficiaries. Bearer shares do not contain the name of the shareholder and are not registered. They can be transferred by physical delivery of the instrument/certificate, and anyone having their possession can encash it. In other words, they are just like currency notes. Nominees of shares, like stockbrokers, can buy and sell the shares without the disclosure of the registered owner of the shares in the case of nominee shareholders. Similarly, a nominee directorship system is used where the name of the real owner is kept hidden.

Figure 18: Money Laundering Cycle
Source: https://www.unodc.org/unodc/en/money-laundering/overview.html

Some of the biggest high-profile money laundering scandals are listed below:

- BCCI (US$23 billion)
- Commerzbank (US$347 million)

- Danske Bank (US$228 billion)
- Goldman Sachs (US$600 million)
- Westpac Bank (US$11 billion)
- Nauru (US$70 billion)
- Standard Chartered (US$265 billion)
- Wachovia (US$390 billion)

4.3.3 Black Money

There is no official definition of black money, but the simplest definition could be money outside the tax and regulatory purview and concealed from the tax administration. Broadly it comes from two categories, illegal activities and legal activities but hidden and unreported for taxation. Obviously, it is hard to quantify the amount of money that is hidden. The participation of black money in the system, besides penalising genuine taxpayers, also undermines the integrity of the country, creating an uneven playing field for the majority of small businesses. If the participation of black money goes unchecked for a long time, it can lead to dangerous dynamics.

4.3.4 Corporate Bailouts

In case of crises like the COVID-19, depression, war etc., corporation bailouts have become a norm around the world. This system of bailouts is fundamentally flawed and goes against the basic principles of free-market capitalism. Moreover, due to globalisation and the interconnectedness of economies, the crisis quickly engulfs the whole world (Hanna, T., 2019, August 24). In a way, these bailouts should be seen as privatising the gains and socialising the losses to the public (Bhandari, R., 2013, March 1). This effort to sustain capitalism through government intervention by pumping trillions of dollars of taxpayers' money into the capital market is a daylight robbery of the public exchequer. This practice is, in fact, an indication of the gross failure of capitalism and the capitalist system is plagued with fraud and scandals.

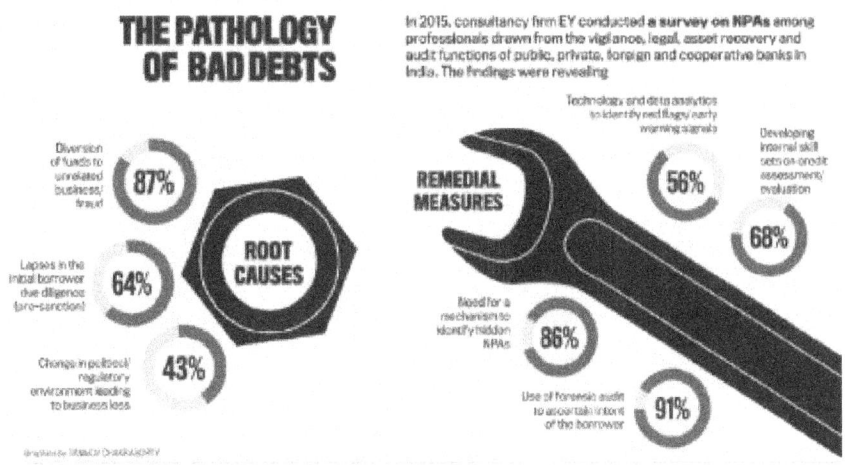

Figure 19: Pathology of bad debts
Source: Tanmoy Chakraborty

The exuberance of the Modi Government to formulate market-friendly policies precipitated a surge in the credit market in India, for which the Indian banking system was ill-equipped and unstable. The over-extension of lending fuelled dangerous speculations and, as a result, necessitated the bailout of YES Bank, India's 5th largest bank, in 2020.

The financial crisis in India started from the Non-Banking Finance Companies (NBFC) that are so designed that they can avoid the regulatory regime that the traditional banks have to go through. These NFBCs raise money from commercial banks (regulated regimes) and invest in high-risk areas like real estate and auto finance. The problem started when Infrastructure Leasing & Financial Services, an NFBC, started cracking up in 2018, and it had to be bailed out by the government. The Indian government did not take it seriously and ended up doing some cosmetic and headline-friendly measures like replacing the board members and executives (Sidhu, A., 2020, April 6). 2018 saw the exodus of diamond trader Nirav Modi from India, leaving behind INR 114,000,000,000

(Mahurkar, U., & Punj, S., 2018, May 10), his uncle Mehul Choksi $2.0 Billion, Liquor Byron of United Breweries, and Vijay Mallya's $1.3 Billion in Non-performing Assets (NPA).

In the US, about 40% of the companies receiving $4 million as a bailout under the Paycheck Protection Program did not pay any corporate tax last year (Bergin, T., 2020, May 28). Companies, including Baker Hughes, Chanel, CNH Industrial, and Easyjet, availing of the Covid Corporate Financing Facility from the UK government are well-known links to tax havens.

4.4 Bretton Wood and the Economic theory - the formation of the World Bank and International Monetary Fund (IMF)

After World World War II ended, 730 delegates from forty-four Allied countries and military coalitions formed during World War II (1939-45) to fight Nazi Germany led front, popularly known as Axis Powers, met in United Washington Hotel at Bretton Woods, New Hampshire USA, with the sole objective to regulate the International Monetary and Financial order from July 1-22, 1944 and established two entities, the World Bank and International Monetary Fund (IMF).

The World Bank is, in fact, a collective name for the three organisations, namely International Bank for Reconstruction and Development (IBRD), International Finance Corporation (IFC) and International Development Association (IDA). The World Bank is meant to advance loans and grants to the governments of low-income countries to undertake capital projects and reduce or eliminate poverty. Though it has 373 member countries, the US, Japan, China, Germany and the UK have the most voting power.

The International Monetary Fund (IMF) was established in parallel with the World Bank at the same conference at Bretton Wood in 1944 and started functioning on December 27, 1945, with its headquarters in Washington, DC. It was primarily established on the ideas of Harry Dexter White (October 29, 1892 – August 16, 1948), a senior official in the US Treasury Department who helped set the American Financial Policy for the Allies and John Maynard Keynes (5 June 1883 – 21 April 1946) an English Economist who fundamentally changed the ideas of the theory of macroeconomics and economics policies of the governments. Incidentally, Henry Dexter White was later accused of espionage for passing information to the erstwhile Soviet Union (Tanenhaus, S., 2011). John Maynard Keynes is the founder of a school of thought of Keynesian economics.

John Maynard Keynes spearheaded a revolution in economic thinking during the great depression of the 1930s, challenging the ideas of neoclassical economics and emphasising and promoting the ideas of the free market for the benefit of workers in the long run. Keynesian principles of economic theory suffered a blow in the 1970s because of the stagnation in Anglo-American economies.

Milton Friedman, one of the intellectual leaders of the Chicago School of Economics thought, an Economist and Statistician, has been a critic of the Keynesian theory. He got a Nobel Prize in economics in 1976 for consumption analysis, monetary theory and stabilisation theory- a set of measures to stabilise the economy and the financial system. In 1999 the Times magazine included Keynes among the most important people of the century, stating that his idea of governments spending money they don't have saved capitalism.

Milton Friedman challenged and criticised Keyneslan economics of demand and supply in favour of the monetarism school of thought, which emphasises the role of governments in controlling money circulation. In the mid-1970s, he tilted towards the neoclassical macroeconomics school of thought that emphasised the importance of rigorous foundations based on rational expectations.

In addition to the WTO, there is another similar organisation with the lofty goals of enhancing the status of the world by involving business, governmental, academic, and other leaders of society in shaping global, regional, and industry agendas, the world's wealthy elite proposed the World Economic Forum.

4.5 World Economic Forum (WEF)

The World Economic Forum is an international not-for-profit, a non-governmental lobby group of elites in Geneva, Switzerland, was founded on January 24, 1974, by Klaus Schwab, a German Engineer and an economist. It is funded by its 1000 billionaire member corporations that have more than five billion US dollars in turnover. It enlists the foremost political, business, cultural and other prominent leaders of society to shape global, regional and industry agendas as its mission on its website.

It convenes its annual meetings spread over five days in January at Davos, a resort in the Alps mountains in Switzerland. The meeting is attended by about 3000 paid members and some selected participants, including investors, business and political leaders, economists, celebrities and journalists, to discuss various issues in 500 sessions.

The forum thinks that the global community can be best managed by a coalition of multinational corporations, governments and civil society organisations. It has named this initiative a Global Reset. It intends to seize the global instabilities, like financial crises and COVID-19 pandemics, as opportunities to promote its agendas as envisaged and in tune with the Shock Doctrine principles explained in the book by the same name Naomi Klein, covered elsewhere in this book under Shock Doctrine.

The nuptial agreement of signing a memorandum of understanding between the WEF, a consortium of corporations and the United Nations for cooperation and coordination to work together in the areas of education, women, finance, climate and health has set a wrong precedent and bad taste. On the face, it may appear to be a benign or rather sound beneficial act to cooperate in the listed areas and ideals, but it will set a wrong precedent for allowing setting up and establishing a base and providing a space for multinational corporations in the UN as there are no such provisions of providing a space in the UN for civil society, for academics, for religious leaders, or for youth (Gleckman, H., 2019, July 3) on the lines it has provided to WEF.

It is nothing less than a mockery to learn about the world's filthy rich getting together annually, arriving in private jets at the luxury ski resort at Davos in Switzerland to express their anguish and concern about the growing poverty, inequality and climate change.

Its ambitious project, Global Redesign Initiative (GRI), proposes switching from an intergovernmental decision-making system to multi-stakeholder governance, a new name for corporate world governance. Ironically, these initiatives have coincided with the increasing indebtedness of the poorer countries.

4.6 Indebtedness, a Political Weapon

A country's debt is measured as the debt to GDP ratio of its public debt to its economic output. The higher the figure, the higher the risk of the country defaulting on repayment and the chances of a financial crisis and collapse of the economy. While a country may owe a debt to other countries at the same time, it may be holding other countries' debt that it may extend a loan to some other countries. In that case, the net international debt of that country is an external debt owing to other countries minus the external debt of other countries.

While researching the net international debt position of various countries, I was led to a page displaying Net International Investment Position (NIIP) position instead (Figures 20 & 21), thereby making you believe debt is an investment. This is nothing less than makeup or plastic surgery; the terms like debt are not only avoided but laced with sugar. NIIP is a measure of a nation's financial condition indicative of its creditworthiness. A nation with a positive NIIP figure is an overall creditor nation, while a nation with a negative NIIP figure is a debtor nation.

Countries and regions	Date	GDP[3] (US$MM)	Date	NIIP[4] (US$MM)
United States	2021	22,675,271	2021Q1	-14,320,275
Spain	2021	1,461,552	2021Q1	-1,096,594
France	2021	2,938,271	2021Q1	-889,171
United Kingdom	2021	3,124,650	2021Q1	-802,202
Ireland	2021	476,663	2020Q3	-705,962
Australia	2021	1,617,543	2021Q1	-664,900
Mexico	2021	1,192,480	2021Q1	-586,528
Brazil	2021	1,491,772	2021Q1	-460,181
India	2021	3,049,704	2021	-379,300
Greece	2021	209,857	2021Q1	-352,272
Turkey	2021	794,530	2021Q2	-280,624
Indonesia	2021	1,158,783	2021Q1	-268,597
Poland	2021	642,121	2021Q1	-254,623
Portugal	2021	257,391	2021Q1	-246,961
Egypt	2021	394,284	2021Q1	-209,599
Colombia	2021	295,610	2021Q1	-171,915
Romania	2021	289,130	2021Q1	-121,438
Pakistan	2021	262,799	2021Q1	-116,935
New Zealand	2021	243,332	2021Q1	-112,488
Peru	2021	225,918	2020Q2	-86,078

Figure 20: List of countries by negative Net International Investment Position (Debtors)

Source: https://en.wikipedia.org/wiki/Net_international_investment_position

It is worth noting that the US tops the debtor's list. In contrast, Japan tops the creditor's list. China is the fourth largest creditor after Japan, Germany and Hong Kong. India is the ninth and Australia's sixth-biggest debtor.

Countries and regions	Date	GDP[3] (US$MM)	Date	NIIP[4] (US$MM)
Japan	2021	5,378,136	2021Q1	+3,375,849
Germany	2021	4,319,286	2021Q1	+3,055,922
Hong Kong	2021	368,633	2021Q1	+2,163,155
People's Republic of China	2021	16,642,318	2021Q1	+2,140,041
Taiwan	2021	759,104	2020	+1,371,420[8]
Norway	2021	444,519	2021Q1	+1,175,781
Canada	2021	1,883,487	2021Q1	+1,105,744
Singapore	2021	374,934	2021Q1	+1,035,082
Netherlands	2021	1,012,598	2021Q1	+959,049
Switzerland	2021	824,734	2021Q1	+808,373
Saudi Arabia	2021	804,921	2021Q1	+587,883
South Korea	2021	1,806,707	2021Q1	+477,517
Russia	2021	1,710,734	2021Q1	+458,533
Denmark	2021	392,570	2021Q1	+278,307
Belgium	2021	578,996	2021Q1	+263,132
Israel	2021	446,708	2021Q1	+190,555
Argentina	2021	418,150	2021Q1	+128,627
Sweden	2021	625,948	2021Q1	+116,427
South Africa	2021	329,529	2021Q1	+97,342
Kuwait	2021	126,930	2020	+89,847

Figure 21: List of countries by positive Net International Investment Position (Creditors)

Source: https://en.wikipedia.org/wiki/Net_international_investment_position

In such a situation, who is in a position to pull the strings? The creditor can not only pull the strings but can also remove the rugs from under the debtor's feet. The situation at national or international levels can not be any different from what happens in society in general as far as the relationship between the creditor and debtor is concerned. It is the creditors who have the upper hand. Given the situation with indebtedness on such a large scale, bankers, regulators, and governments are very well aware that, in the long run, no one's interest is to allow borrowing (Funnell, B., 2009, July 1).

The answer is in capitalism's great dirty secret that this is the only way to let the people be on a spending spree and let wealth accumulate in the hands of the elite. You may often wonder why there is no revolution despite the significant inequality between the rich and the public. The solution for the people is the debt itself; if you can not earn it, you can borrow it. The interest rates are left low to prevent the public from being crippled under the debt burden. Instead of solving the problem, this approach further exacerbates the problem, thereby going into a spiral.

> *"The debt is not only a tool for the economy; it's a political weapon. As the main tool for globalisation, it has disoriented the economy and allowed exportation and extractivism. It is a first-class tool for privatisation of the economy, to end socialism and to create global impoverishment"*
> — Silvia Federici, Emeritus Professor of Social Sciences, Hofstra University, New York, USA.

> *"Public debts are a mechanism of income transfer from the people to the capitalists"*
> — Éric Toussaint, a historian and political scientist (Caponnetto, M., 2022, June 15).

4.7 Climate Bogey, a Ploy to Bolster Corporations

Almost everyone has an opinion on climate change, irrespective of any scientific background in general or climate science in particular, and ready to jump on the bandwagon to be an ambassador of the climate brigade. It is not hard to visualise who is behind this heightened hype and responsible for creating and setting up such an emotive narrative based on the post-truth and who has an axis to grind?

If you fall into this category, I have some questions for you to contemplate and ponder upon. If the climate is changing for bad or good, can you or the politicians change its course? Can you visualise the time-lapse in hours, days, years, centuries, millennia and geological timescale of millions of years? Are you aware of the origin of the earth, the origin of the universe, the origin of life on earth, and the evolution of life propounded by Charles Darwin? Are you aware of why the dinosaurs became extinct and so many other plants and animals are going to go extinct?

Do you know the human race (Homo sapiens) is still evolving, and what form will it take? Do you know marine fossils can be found in the higher ranges of the Himalayas and what it means?

Do you know the continents are still moving, and this phenomenon is called continental drift (Figure 22)? Do you know when it all happened? The human race had not appeared by then yet. Do you know there have been intermittent ice ages indicating that the earth has been warming and cooling in phases? If you had known all this, you would never believe that humans have anything to do with climate change or that humans can ever change the course it is taking or going to take. Enlighten yourself before creating any noise by holding the human race responsible for climate change.

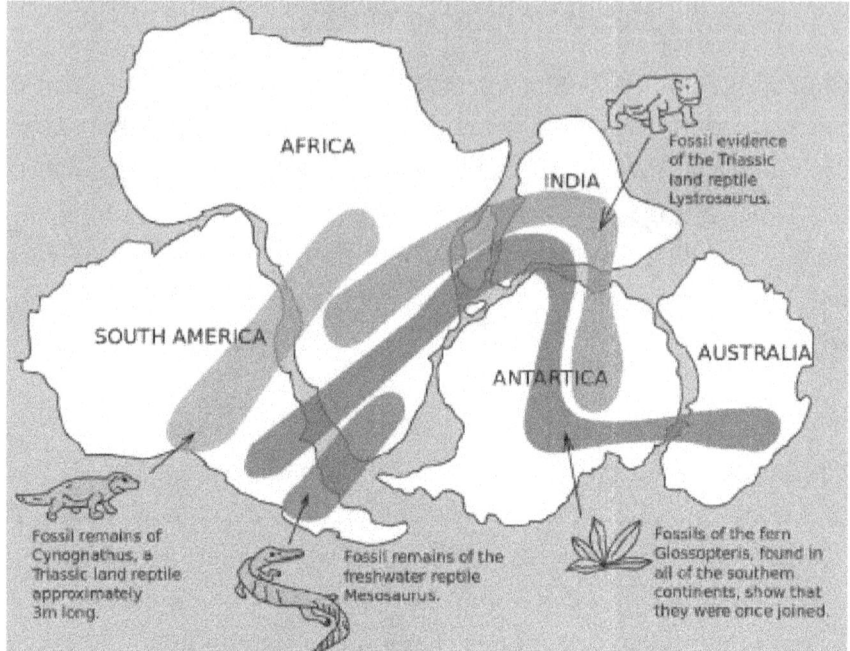

Figure 22: Continental Drift,

Source: https://res.cloudinary.com/dtpgi0zck/image/upload/s---nGTCNxl--/c_fit,h_580,w_860/v1/EducationHub/photos/continental-drift.jpg

If you don't have the capacity, tenacity, time or patience to undertake all the research and find the facts, don't fall prey to the scaremongers. What you can do at best is to try to find out who is going to benefit from this rabble-rousing and who has an axis to grind. It is the corporations who are always looking for opportunities during any calamity like the COVID-19 pandemic to make money and create such bogeys as climate change as a post-truth narrative in case there is no natural calamity.

Plate tectonics and continental drift are a continuing process and lead to new mountain building and submergence of areas and control the climate of the area and sea currents. These changes are minute and take millions of years. Earthquakes and volcanoes are the manifestations of and adjustments to these movements of drifting continents.

The Himalayas, the highest mountain range in the world, was once a sea called the Tethys sea. By the way, the Himalayas are still rising because of the pushing of the Indian plate against the Eurasian plate.

Humans are responsible for air, water and soil pollution, not climate change. The bogey of climate change due to human activity is absurd. It is the creation of either a skewed mind out of sheer ignorance or a shrewd mind out of the cunningness of greedy corporations in connivance with corrupt politicians to scare the shit and fleece the ordinary law-abiding citizens going along with their normal life and finding means and ways to make money from them directly or indirectly by creating and running a scandalous and unconscionable business.

From among the various theories propounded why the focus has narrowed down only to Anthropogenic theory. Because this is the only theory that provides an opportunity to make money by roping in market mechanisms by the corporations in the name of climate mitigation. That is why the carbon markets have become popular policy tools to address the issue of climate change. In his book "Heaven on Earth: Global Warming, the Missing Science (Plimer, I., 2009)", Australian Earth scientist Ian Plimer asserted that global warming is a lie and that the entire international climate science, politics, and media have come together to support this deception.

The carbon trading business is their latest toolkit to create out of the bogey of climate change to generate a new income stream. Carbon dioxide produced by burning fossil fuels is taken care of by the carbon cycle, a simple phenomenon, easy to understand, taught in primary schools.

It is a good idea to innovate and develop alternate sources of energy like wind, solar, tidal, geothermal, hydrogen or nuclear, not because of any danger of climate change but merely because the fossil fuel is of limited quantity and not going to last forever and the demand for energy is going to increase.

Going by the arguments of scaremongers, even if human activity is causing climate change, there is no way they can exercise any control on its course by levying any amount of tax. Surprisingly this lobby had not proposed any plans to counter, arrest or reverse climate change by carbon trading or any other means.

The Carbon market provides an opportunity for investors and corporations to trade both carbon credits and carbon offsets in the garb of the climate crisis and to save the planet. This opportunity was created on December 11, 1997, through the Kyoto Protocols created by the United Nations Framework.

The main objective of the Kyoto Protocol adopted at the Convention on Climate Change was to establish a mechanism to enable trade emission permits. Continuous efforts have since been made to change the public attitude and perception favourable to the industry. As a follow-up of the Kyoto Protocols of 1997, a legally binding agreement was made between 196 participating countries in Paris, known as The Paris Agreement 2015, on 12 December 2015.

In the parlance of the carbon market, CO^2 emission is turned into a commodity by giving it a price tag (Figure 23). These emissions fall into two categories: carbon credit or carbon offset, and both can be bought or sold in the carbon market. The terms carbon credit and carbon offset are generally used interchangeably, but they work on different mechanisms. Carbon credits work as permission slips or quotas to generate emissions, and these permits are usually bought from the government to emit, say, one tonne of carbon. On the other hand, carbon offsets are obtained by removing a unit of carbon from the atmosphere as part of their normal business activity, and they can sell this carbon offset to other companies to reduce their carbon footprint.

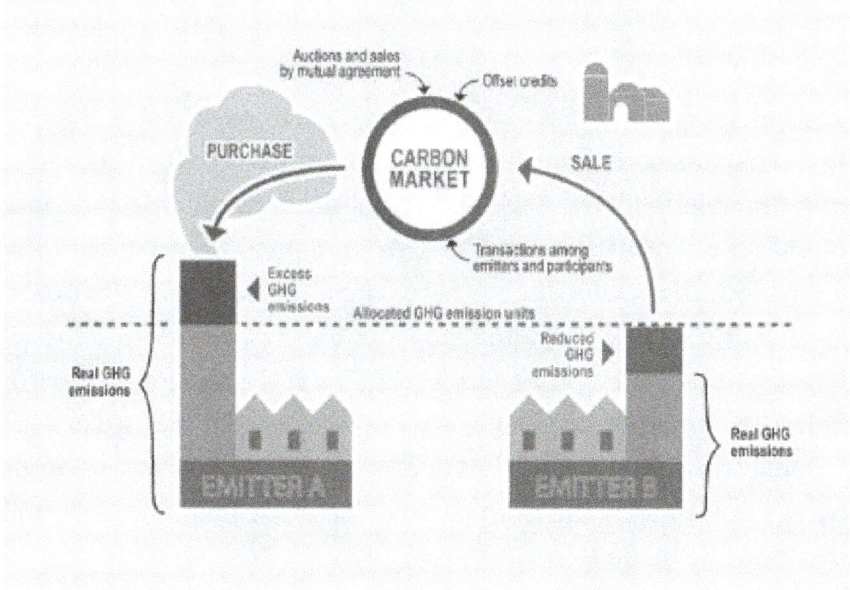

Figure 23: Carbon marketing
Source: https://climatechange.lta.org/

The number of credits issued depends on the emission target set, known as a cap-and-trade program by a particular country. These cap-and-trade programs exist in Canada, the EU, the UK, China, New Zealand, Japan and South Korea. The companies are then incentivised to reduce carbon emissions and stay under their allowed cap.

4.8 COVID-19 Pandemic-a boon for the billionaire

Empty supermarket shelves with no toilet paper, brawls over toilet paper, panic, and bulk buying of groceries became a new normal during the initial days of COVID-19 after the WHO, on March 11, 2020, declared it as a pandemic. It was because of the fear of the impending disaster, the scare, and the dread of the Coronavirus hype created by WHO by sending alarming messages and the media highlighting the famous people getting infected. This hype was complemented by indirect fake news and a very ambitious attempt to contain the virus, enforcement of strict and fierce unwarranted lockdowns.

The basis for establishing and diagnosing Coronavirus was the PCR test (Polymerase Chain Reaction Test) which is a controversial and questionable test. The PCR test establishes the genetic sequence of the virus, not the virus itself. According to a scientific study, coronavirus has always been there, along with other $10x^{13}$ viruses. What was new was the detection kit to detect Coronavirus. This kit has got to be sold all over the world. The hype about Coronavirus helped to create fear psychosis to market this kit and associated paraphernalia. Fat budgets got allocated, and money was set aside by all countries for the Coronavirus. This hype had its eye on this money to be made (Figure 24).

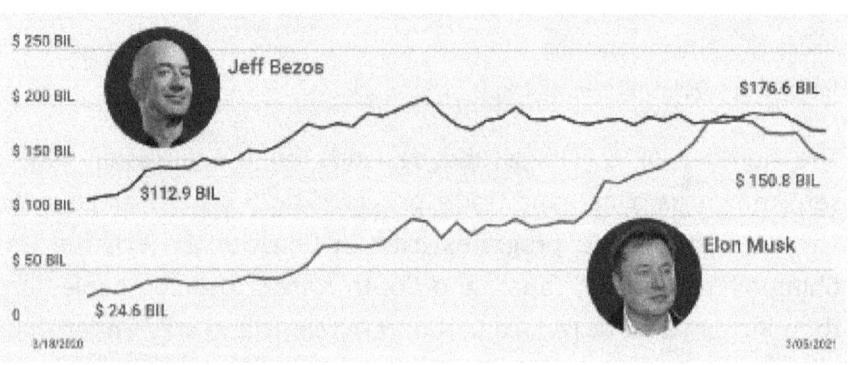

Figure 24: COVID-19 Gainers;

Source: https://media-s3-us-east-1.ceros.com/forbes/images/2021/04/02/1e3c26d14 a22680f75f5e249e92d03f9/billie-timeline2021-bezos-vs-musk.png?imageOpt=1&fit= bounds&width=918

In the case of most viral infections, treatments can only help with symptoms while you wait for your immune system to fight off the virus. No virus can stay in your body for more than 72 hours. It gets killed when you develop a fever.

4 Incapacitation of Capitalism

You may be aware that HIV was discovered in 1984. At that time, the US and France signed an agreement that all HIV-related treatment would be done by them only. To your surprise, till now, there is no record of published scientific research papers proving the presence of HIV in humans and establishing any deaths from HIV. The deaths attributed to HIV happened due to AIDS (Acquired Immunodeficiency), which is a condition, not a virus.

At that time, the two partners were the US and France and the background and the testing ground was South Africa. Thabo Mbeki, the then President of South Africa, criticised the scientific consensus that HIV does cause AIDS. In 2000, he organised a Presidential Advisory Panel regarding HIV/AIDS, including several scientists who denied that HIV causes AIDS. He instituted policies denying antiretroviral drugs to AIDS patients.

This time, the testing ground is China, a secret society, and no one will be able to revolt and expose the sinister game like Mbeki. China's trade is suffering at the moment, and China has been playing the victim. It was learned that the US was trying to do some biological warfare experiments in Wuhan, China. China is reported to have discovered some equipment in the backyard of the US Consulate in Wuhan, and China is investigating it.

Although a random snake-selling wet market in Wuhan is blamed for the virus, the US government seems to have far more to do with it, as the US holds the patent regarding coronaviruses and vaccines.

How many people have died so far due to Coronavirus, a fraction of the number dying every day due to other causes? For example, about 1,500,000 (1.5 m) deaths occur around the world per year in Tuberculosis. TB is 1000 times more dangerous than Coronavirus. Approximately 17,000,000 (17 m) persons die of infectious diseases every year in the world.

You may ask why so many people are dying from Coronavirus. They don't die from Coronavirus, but the fear psychosis thus creates the underlying health conditions. This is called the nocebo effect. For example, if I say you have tested positive for Coronavirus, you may start experiencing the same symptoms as of COVID-19 (Daniali, H., & Flaten, M. A., 2021).

CoronaVirus has rebooted our lives and reformatted our mindset. It has grounded us and brought us face-to-face with realities. It has made all religions at par and re-humanised us. CoronaVirus has tripped off the safety switch, taken control of climate change, made us reconcile with the genders we are blessed with, and evened out our grouses and grumbles. It has bulldozed our pride and prejudices, exposed us and shown us the mirror and has us grappling for the last straw to keep afloat.

Figure 25: Global COVID-19 pandemic-opportunities for the big pharma industry
Source: https://www.tni.org/files/covaxmsi-1.png

No doubt, there will be a tremendous and tumultuous shake-up, reshuffle and realignment in thinking and approach. This pandemic will be a watershed and major marker in human history. This is going to change the rules and modes of the game of power being played at the international level to survive, lead and dominate and reposition in the ever-changing new world order of political power.

The People's Vaccine Alliance has found about nine new billionaires on the Forbes Rich List by investing in vaccine production. Of the 500 new billionaires added to the rich list during the pandemic, 205 come from China, ninety-eight from the US, twenty-six from Germany, Canada and India. While the wealth of the wealthiest and the number of billionaires increased, at the same time, the poor keep struggling with soaring prices and debt, according to a study by the not-for-profit organisation Oxfam.

5 Metamorphosis of the Monetary System

5.1 Background

The monetary system is where the governments provide money supply in the country's economy. Treasury, mint and banks are parts of the monetary system. Money is essential and fundamentally the core of the monetary system. Money has successively evolved from commodity money, commodity-based money, to fiat money over time. Nowadays, it is moving toward digital money and then to cryptocurrency.

The history of commodity money goes beyond centuries, and it is almost impossible to determine when it originated. Commodity money is a physical commodity with an intrinsic value that can be traded off or exchanged for some other commodity or service. Basically, commodity money has four characteristics: durability, divisibility, exchangeability and rarity. On the other hand, commodity-backed money, also known as representative money notes, is issued by banks with no inherent physical value that can be exchanged for any precious metal like gold, known as the gold standard monetary system. The currently used system being followed worldwide is a fiat money system defined by the central bank and laws enacted by governments as legal tender. This also does not have any intrinsic value.

5 Metamorphosis of the Monetary System

In the last one hundred years, the international monetary system failed three times, i.e. 1914, 1939 and 1971. Each time it ensued, the civil unrest significantly damaged and destabilised the global economy. Now James Richards, the acclaimed author of Currency Wars, shows why another collapse is rapidly approaching—and why nothing less than the institution of money itself is at risk this time. (Rickards, J., 2014)

Since World War II, the US dollar has been the global reserve currency. Its failure at any time will surely doom the entire international monetary system, apparently. No other arrangement or option is visible at the moment under such circumstances in case such a situation arises. Optimists have always believed, in essence, that there's nothing to worry about, as the confidence in the dollar will never truly be shaken, no matter how high the American national debt or how dysfunctional the government becomes. With the latest developments at the international level and the advancements of technologies like the emergence of cryptocurrencies, the risk is enormous.

While Washington is gridlocked and unable to progress on its long-term problems, its biggest economic competitors, like China, Russia, and the oil-producing nations of the Middle East, are doing everything possible to end U.S. monetary hegemony. There are reports of China building a Yuan currency reserve teaming with Indonesia, Malaysia, Hong Kong, Singapore, and Chile in collaboration with the Bank for International Settlements (Rosen, P., 2022, June 27). These developments indicated the possible future of money, which has been evolving since its inception centuries ago.

5.2 The Money

Money in whatever form, a piece of metal, a piece of paper or a string of electronic codes, does not have its own value. Its value depends on the importance the people place on it. It is a medium of exchange, a unit of measure to measure wealth. Currently, a total of USD 420 trillion of money is estimated to be circulating in the world (António, H.-O., 2021, June 22). The terms money and currency are often used interchangeably, but money is an intangible item, while currency is the tangible and physical manifestation of money. The transition from coins to paper money took place around 700 AD in China, while parts of Europe kept using coin money until the sixteenth century. The 21st century brought two new forms of currency: the mobile payment system through mobile phone technology and virtual currency like Bitcoin, released in 2009 (Redman, J., 2017, October 31). As of November 2021, a total of 1.03 Trillion USD is understood to be circulating in Bitcoin in the world (Reiff, N., 2022, July 13). With the entry of digital currency, a new chapter is being written in the history of money.

5.3 Digital Currency

Fiat currency is backed by the government that issued it, as opposed to gold or silver. Unlike commodity money, the value of fiat currency is defined by the relationship between supply and demand and the stability of the government that issues it. Fiat money could be in the form of paper currency, coins, or digital cash. Digital Currency is an electronic version of physical currency notes issued and backed by a central bank.

The Reserve Bank of India has announced the launch of a digital form of currency in 2023, and it can be exchanged for paper currency once launched. It is understood that digital currency will exist in parallel with paper currency and can be interchanged and controlled by the Reserve Bank of India. This type of digital currency can be called Central Bank Digital Currency (CBDC). Central banks worldwide are gripped by the issue and grappling with familiarising themselves with the bits and bytes of digital currency and harnessing the technology. CDBCs are gaining momentum as they are safer, more resilient, have greater access, and lower cost than private digital currency. According to the Atlantic Council, ten countries have fully launched a digital currency, viz., Bahamas, Jamaica; Saint Kitts and Nevis; Antigua and Barbuda; Montserrat; Dominica; Saint Lucia; Saint Vincent and the Grenadines; Grenada and Nigeria. Except for Nigeria, the rest of them are Caribbean island countries. About 100 countries are at different stages of development in their efforts to introduce and implement CDBC.

Bahamas introduced Sand Dollar as its CDBC and has been in use for almost over a year (Georgieva, K., 2022, February 10). Chinese CBDC RMB continues to progress at a greater pace as over one hundred million individuals have used it for transactions. But none of these initiatives seems to challenge the emergence of cryptocurrencies.

5.4 Cryptocurrency

Digital currency differs from cryptocurrency as it is controlled and issued by central agencies, whereas cryptocurrencies are not controlled by any central agencies. Cryptocurrency is a digital or virtual currency where transactions are verified, and records of these transactions are maintained by a decentralised system of public ledger called Blockchain, using cryptography. It does not have legislated or intrinsic value and does not have any issuing or regulatory authority like the current monetary system of the Treasury and Reserve Bank, as in the case of prevailing fiat currency. Unlike the banking system, this distributed public ledger is a peer-to-peer digital payment system where anyone can send and receive money from anyone anywhere. You need a digital wallet to store cryptocurrency.

PayPal, better known for money transfer and other services, has only recently allowed customers to trade crypto within their existing accounts on their platform.

In the case of conventional fiat currencies, the trust is vested in and ensured through the money supply issued by a central authority, while in the case of cryptocurrencies, the trust is vested in blockchain technology. Since 2017, cryptocurrency startups have raised over $20 billion via Initial Coin Offerings (ICOs), the equivalent of Initial Public Offerings (IPOs) in the Stock Market, according to a recent study by Autonomous Research (Alexandre, A., 2018, October 10). Despite their widespread usage, benefits and exponential growth, cryptocurrencies remain widely misunderstood, probably because of the perception that crypto investments are risky. However, it is just a matter of time before the current monetary system will get completely replaced with cryptocurrency.

Bitcoin has been around since 2009. However, cryptocurrencies and other applications of blockchain technology are emerging, and more uses are expected in the future. Transactions, including bonds, stocks, and other financial assets, would eventually be traded using this technology. Generally, you need a minimum of USD one hundred to buy the equivalent value of any cryptocurrency based on the prevalent value at that time.

There are thousands of cryptocurrencies besides the best-known Bitcoin, including Ethereum, developed in 2015 and Litecoin, similar to Bitcoin. Bitcoin was developed by Satoshi Nakamoto in 2009. Litecoin has moved more quickly to develop innovations, including faster payments and processes to allow more transactions; Ripple is a distributed ledger system founded in 2012. Cryptocurrencies are impacting not only the storage of financial assets but also non-financial assets such as paintings and videos.

5.5 Non-Fungible Tokens

Non-Fungible Tokens (NFT) are digital assets secured with cryptographical digital signatures on a distributed blockchain ledger. Cryptocurrencies like Bitcoin and Ethereum are also hosted on this blockchain ledger system. However, cryptocurrencies are fungible items because they can be exchanged or traded for something else of equal or similar value, unlike non-fungible ones. NFTs can not be exchanged with anything of equal or similar value because each NFT item is unique and different from any other NFT item, and no two NFT items are the same. Any digital file, like a JPEG or video, when turned into a token and secured onto the blockchain, can be sold and traded.

NFTs are like digital collector's items, like a physical oil painting, as in the case of a physical collector item. Like physical collector's items, NFTs can be sold, but the creator can still retain the copyrights and will get a percentage on the second and subsequent sales. These transactions are facilitated by the establishment of numerous exchanges.

5.6 Crypto Exchanges

A crypto exchange, or a Digital Currency Exchange (DCE), is a platform, a digital marketplace where you can buy and sell cryptocurrency or convert one cryptocurrency to another or to a fiat currency like US Dollar.

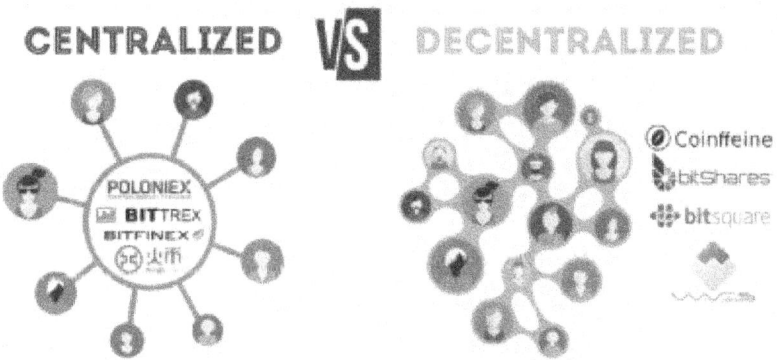

Figure 26: Centralised and Decentralised
Source: https://images.ukdissertations.com/102/0488010.001.png

Crypto Exchange works as an intermediary between buyers and sellers, similar to the Stock Exchange, making money through transaction fees and commissions. Kraken, CoinEgg, Coinbase, Gemini, and Binance are some examples of crypto exchanges.

Basically, there are two types of crypto exchanges, centralised and decentralised (Figure 26). Centralised crypto exchanges act as a third party between the buyer and seller and are more secure and controlled by a company. Currently, 99.9% of the transactions go through centralised crypto exchanges. Some centralised crypto exchanges are Coinbase, GDAX, Kraken and Gemini. On the other hand, decentralised transactions take place on a peer-to-peer basis without the intervention of any third party. Some examples of decentralised crypto exchanges are AirSwap, io, Barterdex and Bloknet.

Name	Last Price	24th Change	Market Cap
BNB	$297.3	-2.27%	$48,477M
Bitcoin	$29,576	-1.63%	$564,175M
Ethereum	$1,761	-3.69%	$212,281M
Project Galaxy (GAL)	4?3	-4.95%	$151M
Green Metaverse Token	1,01	-2.07	$600M

Figure 27: Popular cryptocurrencies as of June 3. 2022 Popular Cryptocurrencies as of June 3, 2022,

PayPal has only recently allowed customers to trade crypto within their existing accounts. There is no single best crypto exchange. It depends on your investment interests and goals depending on the type of cryptocurrency you are trading in as there are numerous cryptocurrencies; Bitcoin is just one being them, depending on the accessibility, security, fees and liquidity etc. Some of the popular cryptocurrencies with the last prices as of June 3, 2022, are given below in Figure 27. The march of cryptocurrencies has been enabled by blockchain technology.

5.7 Blockchain, the Technology

Blockchain is an immutable-shared ledger that forms the underlying technology of the digital platform and supports applications such as Bitcoin. It facilitates the execution, recording and storing of the transactions and tracking the tangible assets like a house, a car, cash or land and intangible assets like intellectual property, patents, copyrights etc., in other words, anything with value. Blockchain is a technological system of recording information that is difficult or impossible to hack and interfere with. It is distributed throughout the network as blocks. Each block contains a set of transactions, and when a new transaction is made, it is added to the system as a new block. Each transaction is recorded with a cryptographic signature called a hash. This system is called distributed ledger technology (DLT) (Figure 28).

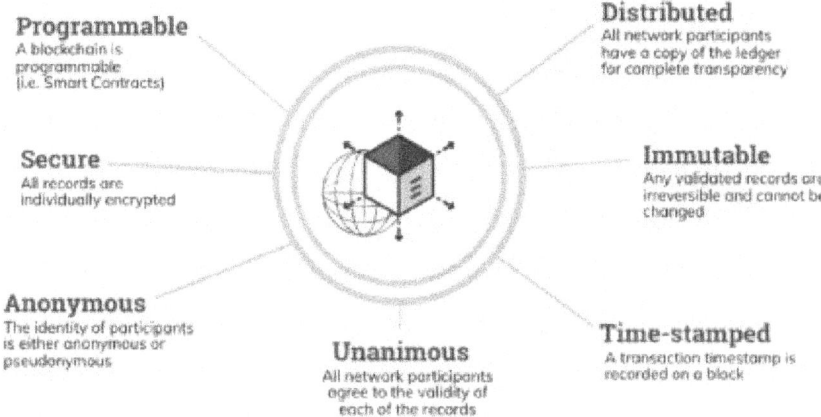

Figure 28: The properties of Distributed Ledger Technology; Source: https://www.researchgate.net/profile/Mrityunjay-Ghosh/publication/355223429/figure/fig1/AS:1079123124457479@1634294410909/The-properties-of-distributed-ledger-technology-39_W640.jpg

Bitcoin is a digital currency launched in 2009 by a mysterious person or a group of people known only by the pseudonym Satoshi Nakamoto. Consider the Blockchain as an operating system like

Microsoft Windows for web applications. Bitcoin just happens to be only one of the items that can be hosted on it. In due course, a lot of business processes are likely to be put on Blockchain because it is economical and efficient and eliminates duplication of efforts and the use of intermediaries.

A next-generation distributed and decentralised internet (Web3) with blockchain as the underlying technology is evolving where anyone can participate without the fear of personal data being stored, sold and traded as in the current system of Web2. In the new Web3 internet ecosystem, no singular entities can control or dominate the system as Facebook and Google do now. In the earlier days of Web1, websites used to be non-interactive static pages.

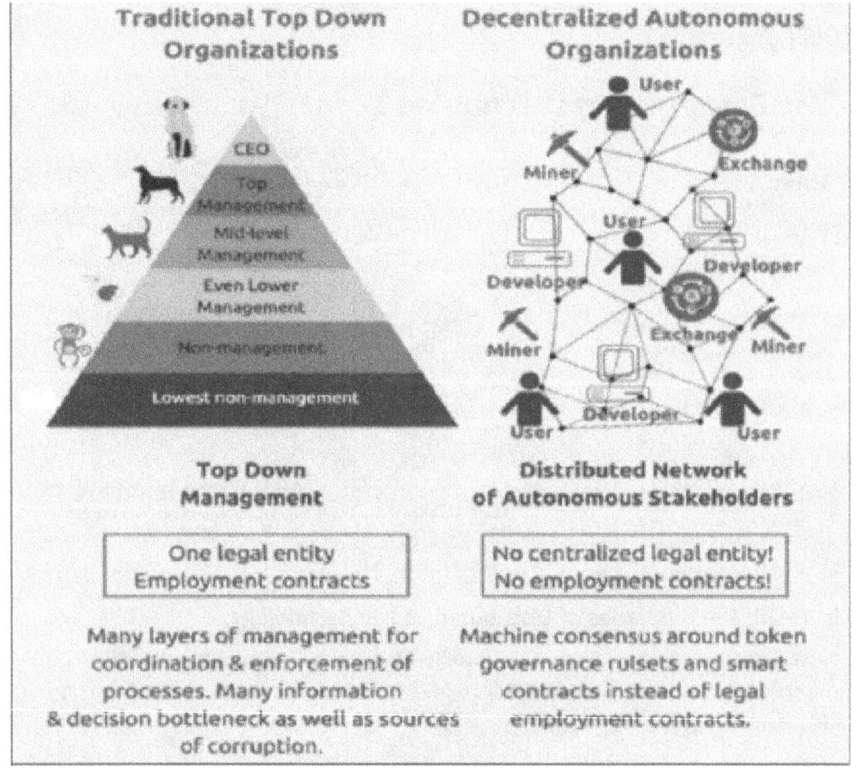

Figure 29: Distributed Autonomous Organisation;

Source: https://sgfs.sitcdn.com/DG/2022/02/04/Delhi/TDG/5_08/33ff8a3e_7742_P_1_mr.jpg

5 Metamorphosis of the Monetary System

Web3 internet will definitely be a disruptive technological revolution as it will break the monopoly and stronghold of a few industrial giants like Facebook and Google because this system will be user-owned, a paradigm shift towards democratisation of the internet.

This decentralised and distributed internet will work like a Decentralised Autonomous Organisation (DAO) (Figure 29) without any central governing body. It differs from the traditional top-down organisation with a hierarchical structure where the organisation is not regulated by any central authority. In this system, the users govern themselves through a self-executing transparent set of software protocols deployed on the blockchain, and the governance is decentralised.

These protocols allow distributed individual entities to make decisions on behalf of the DAO. DAOs are a revolutionary concept in the digital ecosystem. DAOs have three types of members that include investors, employees and customers. So far, DAOs are being used for investment, fundraising and charities, borrowing and buying NFTs directly without the intervention and presence of any intermediaries.

A new buzzword, Metaverse, a term coined by Neal Stephenson in 1992 in the science fiction novel 'Snow Crash' is making rounds on the internet. Metaverse is a multiuser environment merging physical and digital virtuality based on the convergence of technologies enabling multisensory interactions with virtual environments, digital objects and people (Mystakidis, S., 2022).

Top technology firms are vying with each other to enter this area with a bang. Microsoft has acquired Activision Blizzard Inc, a leading company in video games, by spending a whopping USD 68.7 billion. Facebook's exercise of rebranding its parent company and naming it Meta indicates its desire to jump into this arena and focus on the metaverse.

> *"The metaverse is a 3D version of the Internet and computing at large."* —Matthew Ball.

I think it is a crucial life and death situation for Facebook because the advent of Web3 internet and blockchain technology will cause a death blow to its stronghold and make it irrelevant as blockchain technology and DAOs don't allow monitoring by a central authority collecting and selling personal data as per the existing model of Facebook.

All the social media giants like Twitter, Instagram, LinkedIn, YouTube, WhatsApp, Snapchat, Pinterest, Reddit, WeChat and TikTok will end up meeting the same fate. Let me put it, in other words, to clarify what metaverse means. The Cyberspace of Web2 internet will be metaverse on Web3 internet.

Intensive research is still being carried out worldwide to apply Blockchain technology in different applications. Besides cryptocurrency, it has been successively implemented in non-monetary systems like distributed storage systems, proof-of-location, healthcare, decentralised voting systems, and storing and verifying legal documents such as deeds. We can call Blockchain technology a Worldwide Ledger (Miraz, M. H., & Ali, M., 2019, January 31) (WWL). How this technology will impact the global and national monetary systems remains to be seen.

5.8 Cryptocurrency Currency-End of Monetary Sovereignty

The rise of digital currency is another important aspect that is a direct attack and oversteps the concept of sovereignty as it will make monetary sovereignty as irrelevant as territorial sovereignty leading to the new international monetary order. As a result of the switch over from fiat currency to digital currency, the two biggest economies, the US and China, are coming face to face because of their conflicts of interest.

As such, China has completely banned cryptocurrencies and spearheaded the development of Central Bank Digital Currency (CBDC) (Huang, Y., & Mayer, M., 2022). CBDC is the virtual equivalent of a country's sovereign fiat currency issued and regulated by the competent organ of the issuing country as against the cryptocurrencies based on blockchain technologies. On the other hand, the US is devising ways and means to keep its hold and hegemony in its efforts to preserve the existing cross-border financial mechanism of retaining the stronghold of the US Dollar as reserve money for transactions and credit creation. To get an idea of how far the world has moved in this respect, look at the following data. We have 9,516 cryptocurrencies with a total value of USD 1.95 trillion as of March 1, 2022 (Anon., 2022, March 1). About 14% of the world's central banks have already deployed pilot projects to implement CBDC, while 84% actively explore CBDC (Boar, C., & Wehrli, A., 2021, January 27).

China pioneered in issuing its sovereign digital currency and was perhaps prompted because of the fear of private digital currency Diem proposed by the US-based social media giant Meta Platforms (Facebook). Cryptocurrencies have the capacity to de-territorialize money, unlike the government's fiat money, as these are being created, distributed, traded and stored using decentralised blockchain technologies such as Bitcoin. Therefore, Bitcoin or any other similar cryptocurrency can emerge as a global currency beyond the control and beyond the reach of regulatory agencies (Rose, C., 2015). Therefore, it is reasonable to believe that in case of declining confidence in sovereign currencies, people can be tempted to fall back to cryptocurrencies for financial transactions (Williams, M. T., 2014, February 14).

If that happens, the US dollar will no longer be the most important currency in the world. This will lead to the end of the US hegemony that has been in place since the end of World War II. This is because the USD is used as a global reserve currency, a means of payment, and a way to store value.

Though, at the moment, it does not seem to be likely. The only exception is Diem from Meta, formerly Facebook (Brunnermeier, M. K., James, H., & Landau, J. P., 2021). However, none of the countries is favourably disposed to accepting cryptocurrency currency from any private mega technological company. China is hell-bent on internationalising its CBDC currency, RMB, reducing China's dependence on the US dollar-donated global banking system as its long-term goal (Choyleva, D., 2021, July 1). Surprisingly, the US has not yet created a CBDC and is reluctant to regulate Bitcoin either; thereby leaving the field free for private players like Meta to operate.

It would be interesting to watch which way the camel will sit as regards the US-China rivalry in the emerging new monetary world order. Moreover, how this new world order impacts the future of the nation-states.

6 Negation of Nation-States

6.1 Globalisation

Globalisation is a process by which the world is progressively getting interconnected and interdependent. The process of globalisation has been going on since the start of civilisation as the populations have always been migrating for work and better lifestyles. Population migration is generally seen as problematic, and people smuggling is one of the oldest professions besides prostitution. Nowadays, many developed countries have introduced skilled migration policies. This has been necessitated because of the working-age population and skills shortage due to the increasing ageing populations in these countries. Illegal migration is also an ongoing problem in Europe and America, and people smuggling is a thriving business.

Globalisation accelerated in the 18th century because of advancements in transport and communications facilitated by the exchange and integration of ideas, beliefs, cultures and, of course, trade.

Colonialism was started by the Portuguese in the fifteenth century, followed by Spain and then led by England, France and the Dutch Republic, which played an important role in globalisation. The industrial revolution in the nineteenth century set in imperialism that accelerated the pace of colonialism for want of raw materials and markets for the finished products. Many people movements took place due to the devastation and displacement of people during World War I and II.

The introduction of the General Agreement on Tariffs and Trade (GATT) that came into effect on January 1, 1948, for the liberalisation of trade after World War for the economic recovery of the world triggered globalisation. It laid the foundation of the World Trade Organisation, an intergovernmental organisation set up on January 1, 1995, with its head office in Geneva, Switzerland, to formulate, regulate, revise and enforce the rules and regulations of international trade between different countries.

The World Trade Organisation (WTO) was actually supposed to have been formed in 1945 as a third organisation (ITO) along with the World Bank and IMF as part of the Bretton Woods agreement. It could not be formed because the US Congress did not ratify it, as the Democrats lost control despite having their President. GATT was a loose arrangement to cover the gap. After 1945, the Democrats only gained control of all three—the White House, Senate, and House of Representatives—in 1994, leading to the formation of the WTO in 1995. By then, the global situation had changed, and Milton Friedman's theory was challenging Keynesianism. So, it got implemented differently than it was originally conceived.

WTO facilitated trade in goods, services and intellectual rights between member countries in accordance with the trade agreements negotiated and signed between the member states and ratified by their legislatures.

The winners and losers of globalisation can be debated for any length, and the literature is replete with such discussions and debates. But it is hard to find any concrete and solid answer that commits to either side of the argument. But one thing is clear to me that it hasn't worked the way its creators had envisioned or intended. On the other hand, it has worked against them, as they stand to lose significantly. They got an inkling and taste of this during the COVID-19 pandemic. Things have come to such a pass that now it is irreversible though there may be temporary setbacks and hiccups.

Globalisation was probably conceived by the advanced countries that had their manufacturing base and were looking for markets in the developing countries to sell their ware and keep an edge. However, these advanced countries could not envisage the other ramifications that could eventually rather go against them instead of going in their favour.

One of the biggest developments that took place was the whole manufacturing industry moved to China in its entirety; these countries lost their manufacturing base and advantage because of the cheaper labour in China. Instead of the developed countries looking for a market for their manufactured goods, these countries became a market themselves, and China became the manufacturing hub. The developed countries depended badly on China, even for basic and essential supplies. This fact was laid bare because of the COVID-19 pandemic, as because of the shortage of supplies and empty shelves in the shopping centres sent panic waves across the masses. In a way, these countries became self-serving to China. This factor gave China an edge over the advanced countries because of globalisation. In the 1990s, trade barriers between countries were eliminated, and the flow of people, goods, and ideas was liberalised. The rapid advancements in technologies, communication and the advent of the internet revolutionised the world and opened up entirely a new window of opportunity for the business community.

Free Trade Zones, also known as Special Economic Zones, were set up in pursuance of WTO with customs duty exemptions and other local taxes. These zones are specific geographic areas where goods can be imported, warehoused, handled, manufactured, reengineered, redesigned and re-exported. Such zones are usually organised around major seaports and international airports.

Recently technocratic transnationalism has triggered populist reactions within nation-states. This rise of populism and nationalism hampers joint decision-making in the international realm. Blatter, Joachim, and Johannes Schulz (Blatter, J. & Schulz, J., 2022) argue that this conflict between technocratic transnationalism and nationalist populism can be resolved by representative democracies by mutually granting their citizens the right to elect representatives not only in their domestic parliament but also in the parliaments of 'consociated democracies' in tune with the multi-country citizenship.

Consociational democracies are political systems in which different ethnic, religious, or linguistic groups are granted representation and decision-making power in government through a power-sharing system. The power is shared between the executive, legislative and judicial branches of government. This type of government seeks to ensure that all voices are heard and that all citizens have a say in the decisions affecting their lives. This approach aims to promote stability and inclusivity by giving minority groups a say in government and preventing the domination of one group over others. This form of government is intended to promote unity and reduce conflict between different groups within a society.

This type of horizontal and overlapping expansion and extension system of national democracies will bring a three-prong benefit, re-empower citizens in a world of cross-border flows, curb the self-destructive polarisation of party systems and facilitate cooperation among democracies transnationally. They further point out that this approach will encourage Liberal Multilateralism, Deliberative Transnationalism and Republican Intergovernmentalism.

This will also help assuage the feeling of disempowerment and alienation caused among 'globalisation losers' and play an important role in the success of populist demagogues, who put themselves as the leaders of a heroic effort to help people from oppression by 'transnational elites' (Bickerton, C., & Accetti, C. I., 2015). This will give the citizens of participating states the right to elect a certain number of 'consociated representatives' into the parliaments of consociated states, and they will have a say in transnational decision-making.

6.2 Dilution of Sovereignty

The sovereign state is the supreme, absolute, and uncontrollable power by which an independent state is governed and from which all specific political powers are derived; it is the intentional independence of a state, combined with the right and power to regulate its internal affairs without foreign interference. The idea of sovereignty has a long development history and has undergone significant evolution. It has been succinctly dealt with, even by Plato. It has always been closely related to the growth of the modern nation-state. Nowadays, the term is used almost exclusively to describe the attributes of a state—a free and independent state.

The dilution of sovereignty started with the bindings and limitations imposed by the international treaties and laws enacted after the United Nations organisation came into existence, which set the tone for the dilution of the concept of sovereignty.

6.3 Dual Citizenship

Another factor challenging national sovereignties and facilitating globalisation is the emerging phenomenon of dual citizenship. Many countries have introduced dual citizenship, and many people have multiple citizenship. As a result, their loyalty gets divided to multiple countries they happen to avail the citizenship of and the associated privileges that come with dual citizenship. The citizenship of two or multiple countries at the same time may have both advantages and disadvantages, but it definitely dilutes the concept of sovereignty and indirectly aids in making it a step closer to the formation of a transnational state.

Dual citizenship may happen automatically in some situations in some countries, such as when a child is born in the U.S. to parents who are residents of a foreign country, the child becomes a citizen of the US. Dual citizenship can also be obtained through legal processes permitted by many countries.

A lot of countries that allow dual citizenship are Albania, Australia, Barbados, Bangladesh, Belgium, Bulgaria, Canada, Chile, Costa Rica, Croatia, Cyprus, Czech Republic, Denmark, Egypt, Finland, France, Germany, Greece, Hungary, Iceland, Ireland, Israel, Italy, Jamaica, Kosovo, Latvia, Malawi, Malta, Mexico, Nigeria, Pakistan, Panama, Peru, Philippines, Portugal, Romania, Serbia, Slovenia, South Africa, South Korea, Spain, Sweden, Switzerland, Syria, Turkey and the United Kingdom.

The acceptance of dual and multiple citizenships by a number of nation-states is consistently growing over time. This acceptance is a clear signal of the weakening and decline of nation-state sovereignty and the emergence of transnational citizenship or global citizenship. Some states consider it an extension of their sovereignty to promote their national interests overseas through their transborder expatriates (Pogonyi, S., 2011). Growing by this argument, a web of overlapping sovereignty is being created. However, it is a misnomer to consider it an extension of sovereignty, whereas it is a devolution of nation-state sovereignty.

There are many reasons for the de-securitisation of multiple citizenships. Primarily it is the growth of the old age population and declines in the working-age population in the developed countries. This has also been prompted by post-war economic developments and the requirement for a cheaper labour force from third-world countries, as the migrants are reluctant to renounce their original citizenship because of emotional attachment to the countries of their birth. Therefore, the requirement to relinquish their previous citizenship was dispensed with by the receiving countries as an incentive to embrace their citizenship.

Secondly, the changes in taxation laws on the basis of residence rather than citizenship and avoidance of double taxation because of bilateral treaties between various countries also acted as an impetus for the acceptance of dual citizenship.

6.4 Corporate Citizenship

The concept of citizenship is devolving further with the discourse on corporate citizenship in the networks promoting transnationalism. The transnational corporations got a flip, legitimation and liberation from post-1989 free market ideology and, getting a boost from the global networking technology, grew extensively powerful at the expense of nation-states (Castells, M., 2004). Even the richest and most developed nation-states with advanced nation-states are feeling helpless in front of these corporations, while the less developed and smaller nation-states are completely at the mercy of these forces, and their politicians are prone to temptations of corruption and gratifications.

This trend is supplanted by the decline of social support systems like extended families, and trade unionism is increasing a sense of social exclusion in society. This is being manifested in increasing the gap between rich and poor, religious fundamentalism and organised crime (Carroll, A. B., 1998).

The term and concept of Corporate citizenship have been making rounds in the business and academic fields for the last five years. Its usage is growing exponentially (Altman, B. W., & Vidaver-Cohen, D.2000). It could have caught the attention of corporations, particularly because of the negative impacts of corporate operations as a damage control exercise. It is a strange and contentious issue. The more you try to delve into it, the murkier it gets and the more confused you get.

The importance of this concept can be gauged from the amount of attention it is drawing across the world. A number of research centres have mushroomed explicitly devoted to this subject of Corporate Citizenship, to name a few at Boston College in the US, Warwick University in the United Kingdom, Deakin University in Australia and Eichstatt University in Germany (Matten, D., and Crane, A., 2005). Even a dedicated Journal of Corporate Citizenship has come up for this purpose. Most likely, these research centres and the journal are being funded by corporations themselves.

The corporations have already encroached on and subsumed the powers of the states. Now the corporations seem to be up in arms to encroach upon the citizens as they have started claiming themselves as citizens. A joint statement was signed during the World Economic Forum in 2002 by thirty-four biggest multinational corporations, "Global Corporate Citizenship -The Leadership Challenge for the CEOs and Boards". There seems to be an attempt to set a dangerous precedent to encroach on the citizens as per Marsden, 2000 (Marsden, C.T., 2000); 11 and Seitz, 2002 (Seitz, B., 2002), corporations are legal entities with rights and duties in the areas they operate at par with citizens.

Traditionally citizens of a sovereign state are entitled to civil, social and political inalienable rights conferred by the state. Social rights provide the individual with the right to education, health and various welfare etc.; civil rights confer freedom of speech and freedom from abuses and interference by including government and rights to own property, whereas political rights include the right to vote and hold office. From this perspective, it is hard to make any sense of Corporate Citizenship, particularly when corporations have already taken over many roles from the states devolving the democracies into a corporatocracy. In such a scenario, the corporations are supposed to take over the responsibility of the state towards its duties towards the citizens and not appropriate the role of citizenship for themselves. There is a gross conflict of interest as the corporations are driven for profit and not vice versa. It is a very sinister motive of the corporations to subsume the sovereign states as well as the citizens.

The reason behind the corporations getting all too powerful is because of the corporations' influence through lobbying and party funding, primarily added by the excessive indulgence and apathy of the citizens towards voting and not taking an active part and discharging their social responsibility in fruitful political activity.

Instead of being serious about discharging corporate social responsibility towards society in the light of the damage caused by them because of environmental degradation and labour exploitation, the corporations are hell-bent on taking over control of the resources, society and citizens.

6.5 Citizenship for Sale

Many developed countries have implemented policies where anybody who has the money at their disposal can buy Residence by Investment (RBI) or Citizenship by Investment (CBI) of that particular country by investing a particular sum of money; these are called Golden Visa or Golden Passport without going through a typical visa and passport system.

The above table (Figure 30) gives a graphic view of the trend of migration of millionaires availing of this type of visa and their favourite destinations

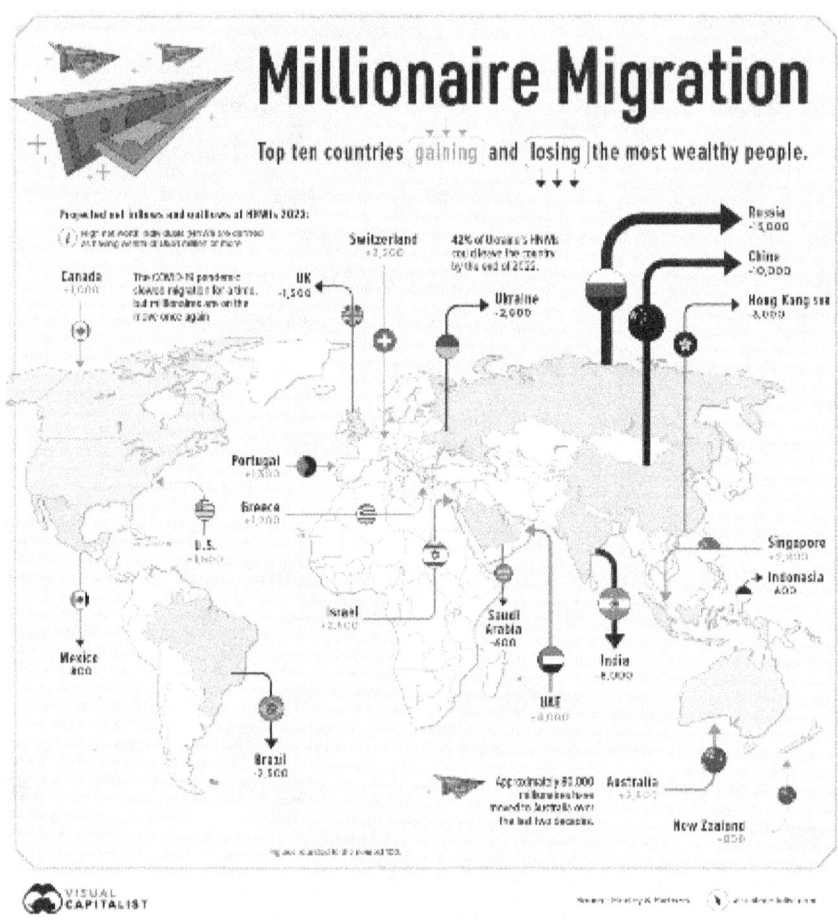

Figure 30: Millionaire migration;
Source: Virtual Capitalist

There is every likelihood of using this visa for financial and economic crimes, including bribery, corruption, tax crimes and money laundering, because of insufficient safeguards (Pavlidis, G., 2021). Some sort of competition between different countries offering this type of migration may further lead to being lenient with such safeguards ending, thereby increasing the chances of this system being exploited for money laundering. According to George Pavlidis 2021, the profit-driven private sector has been found lobbying individual politicians and particular parties to introduce such a visa system. Moreover, the screening process of such applications is discretionary, and such discretionary powers are used to overlook the conflict of interest or the involvement of these politicians in those businesses leaving the field open for corruption. RBI and RCI schemes also have the potential to undermine the efficiency of the automatic exchange of taxation between the countries, increasing the risk of tax evasion.

The countries that provide citizenship by investment are Antigua and Barbuda, Anguilla, Austria, Dominica, Cayman Islands, Cyprus, Germany, Greece, Grenada, Ireland, Malta, Moldova, Montenegro, Portugal, Spain, St Kitts and Nevis, St Lucia, Turkey, UK, United States and Vanuatu. This list is growing. Some countries, like Cyprus, require investment in the local economy, while others require donations to government accounts, like the National Development Fund in Antigua and Barbuda. There are many permutations and combinations in some countries. The amount of investment varies widely, ranging from USD 100,00 for Dominica, St Lucia to over USD 2503950.00 for Cyprus (Langenmayr, D., & Zyska, L., 2021).

Many countries have given a second thought to this provision and are reviewing the system. The UK recently scrapped the investment visa scheme in February 2022 (News, B., 2022, February 16). This scheme was introduced in 2008, and 2,581 visas have been granted ever since to Russian citizens. Australia is also learnt to actively think of scrapping this scheme soon. The EU is reviewing this scheme in view of the Russian-Ukrainian war. Many corrupt public officials and business people have utilised this scheme to conceal their identities and assets.

The data shows that about 40,000 persons have used the RBI or RCI system between 2013 -2019. A maximum number of people have come from China, followed by Russia and the Middle East to some extent.

6.6 Chinese Debt-Trap Diplomacy

"Modern Slaves are in debt, not in chains"-Anonymous

Figure 31: Chinese Debt-trap diplomacy.

Source: https://themeghalayan.com/wp-content/uploads/2022/04/Untitled-design-2022-04-07T013449.796.png

The Chinese Debt-Trap diplomacy further dilutes the concept of the sovereignty of the country under debt, as the nation-states in deep debt can not exercise their free will anymore. Debt-trap (Figure-31) diplomacy is meant to burden the debtor country to such an extent that it creates an unsustainable situation where the debtor is rendered incapable of repaying it back so that it can be pressured to toe the creditor's line to gain a strategic geopolitical advantage. The borrower is directed or manipulated to use the services of the contractors, materials and resources from the creditor country. China has extensively deployed this ploy and has become a cause of concern to the international community. The Chinese stranglehold over international finance is overwhelming, and it is laying this debt trap as a part of its aggressive posture, foreign policy and hegemonic ambitions in the Indian Ocean region. China is feared to use the debt trap as a geopolitical weapon in a trade war. The term debt trap was coined by Brahma Chellaney, an author of nine books on geostrategic affairs and professor of strategic studies at the Centre for Policy Research in New Delhi.

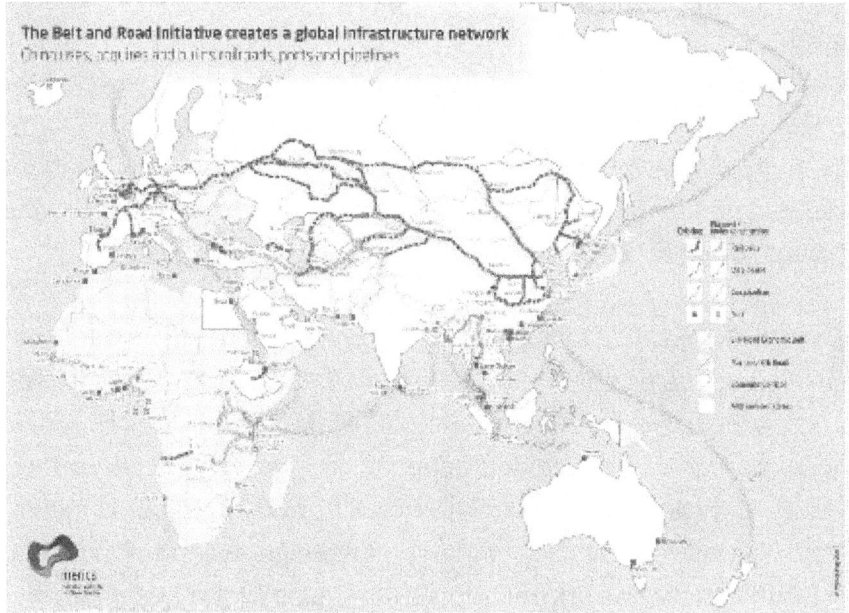

Figure 32: Mapping the Belt and Road Initiative.
Source: The Economist 28July2018,14. https://www.merics.org/en/bri-tracker/mapping-the-belt-and-road-initiative

The dangers of Chinese debt-trap diplomacy are no more hypothetical but real as exposed by the Sri Lankan economic crisis, nationwide protests, rioting, and the associated developments recently emerged as a template for the fallout of China's debt-trap diplomacy as a result of its Hambantota Port that was handed over to China for 99 years lease in 2017. Under such circumstances, Sri Lanka is under debt to equity swap agreement. Lanka is not in a position to resist the usage of its Hambantota Port as a Chinese military base. Hambantota Port is just one of the 3000 such projects financed by China under the Belt and Road Initiative (BRI) commenced in 2013 (Figure 32).

Similar situations are likely to arise in African countries where China has given loans extensively. China has an edge with more leverage as far as institutional resources are concerned compared to individual African countries. African countries seem to have awakened to this danger as they are understood to garner African Union's Institutional support (Van Staden, C., Alden, C., & Wu, Y.-S., 2018). The Lankan predicament has sounded dangerous alarms in many similarly placed situations in small South Asian nations like Bangladesh, Nepal, Maldives, Bhutan and, of course, Pakistan (Raveendran, K., 2022, April 7).

The BRI project, a China state-led capital economic model, has challenged the established market conceptualisation and started an entirely new concept of transnational state capitalism with a dual agenda of profit-making and geopolitical goals (Liu, H., & Lim, G., 2022). This concept is a complete break from the traditional nation-state/interstate financing through sovereign wealth funds and institutional framework of nation-states outreach for hegemony but transnational state-owned enterprises (SOE) outreach for profits and geopolitical agenda.

This practice of Chinese predatory lending through BRI projects to garner geopolitical ends prompted about fifteen US Senators to express their concern about China attempting to weaponize capital not only in Asia and Africa but also Europe. This may lead to debtor countries defaulting on repayment, and IMF would have to intervene to bail them out as Pakistan was bailed out to avoid debt obligation on China-Pakistan Economic Corridor (Lai, K. P. Y., Lin, S., & Sidaway, J. D., 2020).

It is interesting to note that, in a way, this is what the IMF and the World Bank have been doing, extending predatory loans and dictating terms and conditions in return from the debtor countries but on a different scale in an insidious way and as sinister ends as China. The only difference is the IMF and the World Bank are a consortium of many wealthy countries, whereas in this case, China is doing it singularly as a Transnational Corporate State. Moreover, some of the predators have turned into prey. It is difficult to digest for the predators that their roles have been taken over by a much bigger predator. Actually, China has taken over the job of the IMF and the World Bank and rendered them jobless. Hard to believe, isn't it?

7 The Rise of Transnational Corporate Republic

7.1 Tax Havens

A tax haven is a jurisdiction with meagre "effective" taxation rates and complete financial secrecy for foreign investors. While globalisation opened up new avenues for capital flows due to reduced trade barriers, it also started an unhealthy trend of competition in aggressive taxation laws and practices in different countries to attract foreign funds and development. This prompted individuals and companies to exploit this loophole to avoid taxes completely. In the so-called tax haven countries, the tax rates and policies are designed in such a fashion that the same can be manipulated by investors to flout tax rules in their home countries with impunity and anonymity (Jalan, A., & Vaidyanathan, R., 2017).

A tax haven is an offshore country where taxes are levied at a very low rate for foreign investors. No residency or business presence is required to benefit from their tax policies. Additionally, tax havens share limited or no financial information with foreign tax authorities. There is a multitude of small island countries that serve as tax havens, and their economic models are designed to provide such services to corporations to hide their incomes and avoid taxes. As such, these countries have no natural resources or economic activity.

Multinational corporations employ a bunch of expensive solicitors and accountants to manipulate the taxation laws of the countries of their operations, avoid taxes and do not pay any taxes anywhere.

While high-tax countries lose corporate tax revenue from businesses shifting profits elsewhere, tax havens can reduce the cost of financing investment in those countries, indirectly facilitating economic growth. Though tax havens may seem questionable, investing through a trust or company in a tax haven is legal.

The top ten tax havens in the world are Luxembourg, Cayman Islands, Isle of Man, Jersey, Ireland, Mauritius, Bermuda, Monaco, Switzerland and the Bahamas. Luxembourg is considered to be the best tax haven in the world. According to a report from Citizens for Tax Justice and U.S. PIRG Education Fund, approximately 30% of U.S. Fortune 500 companies have subsidiaries in Luxembourg. For example, Amazon funnels all of its sales in Europe through its official European headquarters in Luxembourg.

The Cayman Islands currently hold banking assets equal to one-fifteenth of the world's total $30 trillion in banking assets. In addition to having no corporate tax, the Cayman Islands impose no direct taxes on residents, including property, income, and payroll taxes. The Caymans are especially popular with hedge fund managers because there is no corporate or income tax, even on interest or dividends earned on an investment. These tax havens come in handy for corporations to expand and increase their grip on the nation-states wherever they may have their stakes.

Broadly speaking, there are seven classes of tax havens based on the specific needs of the prospective investor client, as one size does not fit all (Murphy, R., 2008, June 30).

1. Incorporation hubs: for setting up offshore companies with minimal regulations, disclosure and paperwork, as in Montserrat and Anguilla
2. Secrecy jurisdictions: for guaranteed and stringent secrecy of the identity of the persons, such as Liechtenstein, Singapore, Dubai, and Turks & Caicos islands.
3. Specific geographical market suppliers: special offshore entities for particular countries, such as the British Virgin Islands for Chinese, Panama for the US, Jersey for London, and Vanuatu for Australian markets.
4. Specialist service market: for particular industries suiting the nature of operations, such as Bermuda and Guernsey for reinsurance and the Cayman Islands for hedge funds.
5. Market entry conduits: for investing in particular countries by virtue of being a part of some double taxation treaty enabling to save money such as Mauritius for Indians, Netherlands for Europeans.
6. High Net Worth providers: for the wealthiest with a high degree of secrecy, such as Switzerland, London and New York.
7. Low tax regimes: for low tax rates for transfer mispricing, such as in Ireland.

Offshore Finance Centres (OFC)-a Siamese Twin: As opposed to the tax havens, OFCs are a group of specialists of lawyers, taxpayers, taxation experts and bankers in the tax haven countries who provide specialist services to the individuals or companies to help them structure their entities to circumvent ways to exploit the taxation of their home countries. They sell their services to clients. The tax havens and OFCs form the complete offshore world. Apparently, these OFCs are the major contributors to the GDP of the tax countries as these small countries are otherwise devoid of any economic activity or productivity.

Corporations are characterised by the separation of ownership and management. As shareholders are the actual owners of a corporation, they don't have the necessary skills to manage it. As a result, the job of conducting the business of a corporation is done by the Directors as managers, who are elected representatives of the shareholders.

The actual idea behind this arrangement was the belief and understanding that these managers would act in the best interest of the shareholders, but that is not the case, and these managers maximise their own personal wealth instead of the shareholders (Desai, M., & Dharmapala, D., 2009). These managers indulge in tax sheltering practices using tax haven services, and this tax sheltering practice renders the profits and earnings opaque for the shareholders. It is behind this curtain the managers divert the earnings to themselves without the knowledge of the shareholders.

7.2 Corporate State

Globalisation has been initiated, attempted and embraced with the idea of economic development and the economy at its heart. The ramifications of globalisation and its political implications were never given proper thought. With the view of the economy as the focus, the corporations were given a free ride granting them extra and additional leverage to operate and relate over and above the individual citizens. As a result, the corporations kept growing financially, physically and operationally, going international and overseas and starting to attain multinational status.

Various agreements were made between states to leverage each other country's corporations. Many times these international deals of the corporations have been made to look like government-to-government deals, with heads of the states freely lobbying and negotiating with foreign countries on behalf of the corporations. This could only be possible with some underhand understanding between politicians and the corporation, involving some underhanded dealings. As a result, the corporations kept increasing their clout and started competing, overstepping, transgressing and ultimately overpowering the state powers. These symptoms have started glaring openly at us and staring us in the face.

While these corporations blatantly used all the leverage provided by the states and at the same time avoided all their responsibilities towards environmental degradation, tax evasion, human rights abuses etc. but also started influencing and encroaching on the democracies. Corporations have not only become increasingly powerful but also started posing challenges and threats to democracies (Bieler, A., & Morton, A. D., 2014).

Globalisation has drastically changed the international order with the entry of these non-state entries of transnational corporations that have started taking over the core functions of the state. The states seem to have been reduced just as conduits and props of the corporations rendering the states meaningless, helpless and obsolete. The reason is very simple: the political parties of all denominations depend on the corporations for the funds needed for contesting elections; the parties are funded by the corporations, and the governments end up subservient to the corporations. Instead of the governments regulating the corporations and holding them to account, the equation has reversed, and the corporations have now started dictating terms and regulating the governments and getting the governments to pass the rules and regulations that suit them. The corporations employ highly paid lobbyists to ensure the laws are framed in such a way that these multinationals maximise profits regardless of the social costs and environmental damages (Bhandari, R, 2013). The (question thus arises naturally, who is more powerful, the state or the corporations? The answer obviously is the corporations.

Right now, it appears that the rapid pace of globalisation has temporarily slowed. The globalisation process was initially put on hold by Donald Trump's America First campaign, which was launched in response to China's state-led worldwide aggressive growth and its border and road programme. The scenario that has put globalisation on hold has been made worse by the recent Russian intervention in Ukraine.

There is no doubt that corporations wield huge power in international politics. The states are now directly competing with corporations besides other states for influence. Multinational corporations definitely have the edge over the states and are placed in an advantageous position because they have shifted their operations to different countries with weak tax compliance, park their money in tax havens, and use a complex network and web of shell company structures (Heemskerk, E., 2018, July 10).

Basically, governments are designed for the people, by the people, and of the people. They exist solely to do what is in the best interest of the people. Corporations, on the other hand, have the sole objective to maximise their profits with no loyalty to the people. The corporations have their operations in all the countries, ship jobs to countries with cheaper labour and move their corporate headquarters to a P.O. Box in the tax haven Islands countries just to avoid paying taxes. Corporations lead to making a very small number of people extremely wealthy rather than empowering individual citizens.

Thus, the citizens are reduced to merely being cogs spruiking the corporations, unaware and involuntarily left with no other option. When we scramble through the news, we find countries are being referred to merely as economies and their citizenry consumers. It can rather be said that the transnational state thus emerging will be controlled by corporations. It will be a corporate state for all intents and purposes, not a sovereign nation-state.

In democracies, the political parties need to face elections and contest and win elections; they need vast amounts of money. Where does this money come from, large businesses and corporations? These corporations are funding all the parties as they have access to funds of that magnitude at their disposal. Why do these corporations fund them, what for, and what do they want from politicians? In exchange, they get the politicians to frame policies to suit them. Whom are the politicians supposed to be working for? Whose interests are they supposed to serve, their masters, the corporations, not the subjects, the citizens? Thus, as a result, the politicians end up as mere pawns in the hands of corporations, and under such circumstances, they lose their rights to exercise their minds and free will and mortgage their conscience and moral rights to corporate masters. They have no option. For example, about 67% of the questions asked in the Indian parliament's question hour time in the last ten years were related to the requirements of corporations (Bajpai, P. P., 2022).

Moreover, the politicians play just second fiddle to the corporations as forty-three per cent of 198 members who left US Congress between 1998 and 2005 became registered lobbyists and over half of the lobbyists at four of the best-known Brussels lobby consultancies have previous experience working inside EU institutions (Anon., 2012, January 24). So many prominent politicians, after retirement, end up working with corporations as consultants or advisors. These multinational corporations employ a bunch of expensive solicitors and account to manipulate the taxation laws of the countries of their operations and avoid taxes. These corporations end up paying very little or no tax at all anywhere.

Moreover, there is a multitude of small island countries that serve as tax havens, and their economic models are based on providing such services to hide the incomes of these corporations. The shareholders of these corporations, irrespective of their citizenship status, have no moral or social bindings with any countries but only to profits, dividends and bonuses as they possess multiple passports. These citizens can rather be called corporate citizens, not citizens of any nation-state. Theoretically, the concept and definition of 'Corporate Citizenship' stipulate that corporations have social, cultural and environmental responsibilities to the community in which they operate, besides economic and financial responsibility to its shareholders or immediate stakeholders. It, therefore, becomes imperative for corporations to take on social obligations. But why should they do so? They don't have any motivation or regulator; their only motivation is profit. Social obligations fall outside their purview.

The political parties depend on corporations for contesting elections, and the governments of all dispensations end up subservient to these corporations as a result. Instead of governments regulating corporations and holding them accountable, they start regulating the government and dictating the terms.

Transnationalism refers to the spread of economic, political and cultural processes beyond national borders. It has been happening for some time now and is gradually leading towards the formation of a transnational state. It has been initially triggered by globalisation, and its pace has quickened because of getting increasingly interconnected with the free flow of financial as well as human capital across borders. The change is gradual, consistent and irreversible, with a few exceptions here and there.

As the corporations have their operations across borders in multiple countries, so have their shareholder's multiple passports. As a result, the shareholders of these corporations, too, have no moral or social bindings with any country but only to profits, dividends and bonuses, as do corporations.

7.3 Corporatocracy

As a matter of fact, the corporatisation of governments has led to the disempowerment of individuals as the process of governance and decision-making has shifted from the state being accountable to the people to the corporations not being accountable to the people. This fact has been obliquely referred to by David Lane in his paper Global Capitalism and the Transformation of State Socialism (Lane, D., 2009) though in some other context. Therefore, it can be easily deduced that one of the major planks of liberal democracies has crumbled. With this sort of disempowerment of the individuals and the process of governance passed on to the corporations, a new form of governance comes into play that can be defined as Corporatocracy. In other words, we can say that democracy gets transformed or devolved into a corporatocracy.

> *"Fascism should more appropriately be called Corporatism because it is a merger of state and corporate power."*
> – Benito Mussolini

The behaviour of the shareholders over time has also changed, and it has also played a contributory role in the lead-up to this situation in a way. The holding time of the shares has changed from about seven years for long-term investor-years to seven months for short-time speculators rendering the corporation ownerless (Skypala, P., 2009, September 8). That means the shareholders have moved their motive and modus operandi from investor to speculator.

Rather than admitting to and accepting this transformation of democracy into corporatocracy, many peer-reviewed journals and researchers studies, like Fuchs, D., Kalfagianni, A., Sattelberger, J. (2010) (Fuchs, D., Kalfagianni, A., Sattelberger, J., 2010), Schaik, L. G. V., & de Pas, R. van. (2014, July 15) (Schaik, L. G. V., & de Pas, R. van., 2014, July 15) and Kuyper, J. W. (2018) (Kuyper, J. W., 2018) are trying to advocate various explanations for the legitimation of democracy. The corporations, through their stronghold on the media, interest groups and organisations, have cajoled us into believing that there is no other alternative mode of governance (Barbier, C. L., 2017, October 14). There is no way of checking or reversing the politicians; government officials are dishonest and have been held captive by the multinational corporations that enable the rich to get richer and the poor to get poorer.

These corporations use a double edge weapon of advertising to promote their big brands and trademarked products and use the consumers as the tools for the promotion of their products by making us wear their products with the oversized emblems of their brands on our apparel and other display products being displayed prominently.

In a corporatocracy, all economic potential of the country, like natural, financial and human resources, is owned by corporations as the powers of the state are subsumed by the corporation. The only economy for the state to implement implements the imposed budget by controlling and restraining the demands, and the nation-state is reduced to a mere security service or a local police station for the transnational corporation (Bauman, Z., 1998). An idea of the worth of these transnational corporations can be had from the fact that the assets of the top transnational corporations exceed the gross national product of many nation-states; as a result, they are in a position of power to dictate their own agenda to drive the economy in the direction they desire (Shaw, H. J., 2008).

As a result of the passage of power from the nation-states to the corporations, the locus of the identity of the citizens has moved from what they do as a job and their contribution to society to what they consume. Their lifestyle and language led to a new consumer society doctrine because of job insecurity caused by frequent corporate downsizing.

Transnational corporations are successfully legitimising their political authority across the world. A case in point is legalising unlimited corporate election funding as per the Supreme Court decision in

Citizens United vs Federal Elections Commission (130 US 876) in 2010 in the US, reducing democracy to a democratic facade (Wiist, W.,2011, July). Another case in point is the introduction of electoral bonds skillfully crafted to manipulate the regulatory authorities and create a political funding mechanism in India (Vaishnav, M., 2019, November 25), enabling Corporations to fund any amount of money to the political parties totally anonymously. Over and above, this has been touted as an election reform exercise unabashedly and contemptuously.

In the corporatocracy, the enlightenment principle, the government of the people, for the people and by the people with inalienable rights to life, liberty and the pursuit of happiness and private property, is changed to the government of the corporations, for the corporations and by the corporations. The active agents of these corporations include special interest corporate-funded political action committees, lobbying groups, conservative think tanks, politicians and pro-corporate judges. Retired politicians and bureaucrats are recruited as Corporate lobbyists (Doan, P., 2016, April 30).

In Australia, both the main parties Coalition and Labour parties, have been indulging in deskilling the public services by axing the jobs and increasingly depending on consultants for policy advice and expertise both at the federal and state levels, according to Michael West (West, M., 2017, February 20) and inching closer towards corporatocracy. The federal government paid about $2.6 billion over a period of ten years to the big four accounting firms, viz. PwC, EY, KPMG and Deloitte. This included paying about $ ten million to PwC for writing a report on the future burden of welfare costs, and that comes down to $75,000 per page of the report. It's interesting that the same accounting firms act as tax advisors for all multinational corporations around the world, telling them how to avoid paying taxes. This is a clear and obvious conflict of interest. The Investor-State Dispute Settlement Clauses of the now shelved

7 The Rise of Transnational Corporate Republic

Trans-Pacific Partnership (TTP) Agreement had provisions to allow corporations to sue nation-state governments, a sinister move of the corporations to encroach on the sovereign nation-states.

Because of the similar clauses in other trade agreements, about 120 cases have been filed under various trade agreements; Veola sued Egypt for lifting the minimum wage, and the tobacco giant Philip Morris sued Australia over plain cigarette labelling.

Similarly, if implemented, the proposed Transatlantic Trade and Investment Partnership (TTIP) would have enshrined the corporations to restrict future governments from overturning the changes under International Law. These two agreements, TTP and TTIP, were an attempt to tilt the balance of power between corporations and the states towards corporations to create effective corporatocracy (Kitty, J., 2013, December 6).

Thomas Rivas (Rivas, T., 2020, October 18) argues that corporatocracy is a build-up of a new global empire being built using more subtle economic tools against the openly militant methods used for colonial empire building in the past in building the Roman Empire or British Empire. John Perkins (Perkins, J.,2004) beautifully elucidates the story of the rise of corporatocracy in his book, "Confessions of an Economic Hit Man".

> *Economic hit men (EHMs) are highly paid professionals who cheat countries around the globe out of trillions of dollars. They funnel money from the World Bank, the U.S. Agency for International Development (USAID), and other foreign "aid" organisations into the coffers of huge corporations and the pockets of a few wealthy families who control the planet's natural resources. Their tools include fraudulent financial reports, rigged elections, payoffs, extortion, sex, and murder. They play a game as old as empire, but one*

that has taken on new and terrifying dimensions during this time of globalisation. I should know; I was an EHM.

– John Perkins, Confessions of an Economic Hit Man (2004)

7.4 State Corporation

Getting a cue from this development of corporations increasing their hold over the sovereign states, directly and indirectly, and using its business acumen, the Chinese State smartly preempted this move of the corporations and stepped in the shoes of a corporation itself and started acting like a corporation. Having a single-party structure and closed system gave it an edge over other states to try a similar model.

Keeping in view its objective and far sight, it started laying the debt traps for smaller and insignificant states and, through its belts and roads initiative, started throwing money and buying stakes in various corporations. As a part of this strategic move, It also started buying infrastructures and large chunks of land in various sovereign states. It played its cards quietly before anyone could sense its move and judge its motive. It has now reached such a state that it has already started being overawed in the world with its financial prowess and military might.

China has even infiltrated other sovereign states by buying the politicians of different parties in different countries either by financing their elections or just bribing them to lobby for its interests in those sovereign states. China will likely be heading the global economy with 55.1 trillion surpassing the US by 2036 (Amoros, R., 2022, June 13).

As a result, China has gone a step further from being a corporate state as most democracies are halfway through devolving into corporate states, whereas China has emerged as the State Corporation.

The state-led investments in China are a new and natural corollary of globalisation (Babic, M., Garcia-Bernardo, J., & Heemskerk, E. M., 2019).

For a long time, the Western governments, probably, because of their overconfidence, thought their model of governance was superior to others and, as a result, were tempted to assume that China would one day seamlessly merge or co-exist in the international system and fail to understand the emerging trend. Particularly after China acceded to joining the World Trade Order in 2001, the western countries were made to believe in such an assumption and got more complacent. Incidentally and surprisingly, most existing literature on this subject is written from the US and Western countries' perspectives.

With Xi Jinping assuming power in 2012, China seemed to take a different course of supremacy and control of the new world order rather than accepting the hegemony of western democracies. Such a vision of supremacy comes from and is deep-rooted in the Leninist idea of power and domination.

China has increasingly been involved in massive transnational investment deals like China-led ChemChina (China National Chemical Corporation), a Chinese State-owned chemical company investment of $43 billion to take over Swiss agrochemical giant Syngenta in May 2017. Syngenta, a leading global provider of agricultural science and technology, particularly seeds and crop protection products, has headquarters in Basel, Switzerland, and further locations in Chicago, Tel Aviv, and Shanghai were taken over by China.

The consequences of the emerging phenomenon of cross-border state-led investment need to be studied in the context of the transnational corporate state (Babic, Milan, et al.2019) and the dilution of the concept of the sovereign state. These transactions happened in the form of states acting as investors in corporations worldwide.

Though besides China, there are some other examples of State-led transnational investments like Rosneft's, a Russian integrated energy company headquartered in Moscow, $13 billion deal to take over India's Essar Oil in August 2017. The Home Security and Intelligence Agencies in India raised security concerns about the geopolitical impacts of the Rosneft deal and red-flagged it (The Asian Age, 2017).

This type of investment is called Foreign Direct Investment (FDI). These cases illustrate how state-led foreign investment is more than a normal FDI transaction. It may and often does cause insecurity and political concerns. Especially when authoritarian regimes like China engage in outward economic expansion through FDI, geopolitical implications can not be ruled out.

The above-mentioned cases are no exception. There is a rapid rise in the number of such investments and global activities of Sovereign Wealth Funds (SWFs). SWF is a state-owned investment fund that invests in real and financial assets such as stocks, bonds, real estate, and precious metals or alternative investments such as private equity funds or hedge funds (Karolyi, G. A., & Liao, R. C., 2017). These types of state-led foreign investments challenging traditional ideas of sovereignty and state power (Dixon, A. D., & Monk, A. H. B., 2011) have rendered the idea of territorial sovereignty irrelevant. Similarly, the emergence of blockchain-based cryptocurrencies is demolishing monetary sovereignty, one of the key tenets of sovereignty (de Caria, R., 2019).

The term transnational state (TNS) was coined by sociologist William I. Robinson (2001), who claims that a nascent political, juridical and regulatory network is coming into existence worldwide as an outcome of globalisation. The setting up and establishment of the World Trade Organisation (WTO), coupled with the increasing number of Free Trade Agreements (FTAs) and International & Bilateral Investment Agreements (IBIAs), have led to global corporate rule in the preceding decades in the wake of globalisation.

Many agreements have instituted and incorporated an Investor-State Dispute (ISDS) mechanism allowing corporations to sue states for discriminatory policies, any true or perceived loss of profit or interpretation of contracts in the International Arbitration Courts with the provision of imposing enormous financial penalties to the states. These types of provisions in the agreements directly and effectively dilute the powers of the state while increasing the powers of the corporations at the same time. This has set a trend of empowering corporations vis-à-vis the states. Moreover, the annual revenues of some corporations are more than the gross domestic product of many countries. Global financial institutions like the International Monetary Fund (IMF), World Bank, and International Financial Instruments also give more leverage to corporations through their policies. The other factors that go in favour of the corporations are various tax breaks and other tax evasion and tax avoidance mechanisms.

According to Sean McGoey, there is an annual loss of $500 billion due to corporations as per the State of Tax Justice 2021 report (McGoey, S., 2021, November 19). Corporations can also gain more economic and political power through the practice of mergers and acquisitions. For example, the merger of three giants, Bayer-Monsanto, ChemChina-Syngenta and DuPont, obtained virtual global control of the seeds and agrochemicals.

7.5 Transnational Corporate Republic

Democracies are slowly but surely sliding towards corporatocracy, where the economic, political and judicial systems are controlled either directly or indirectly by corporate interests. The idea of corporation bailouts, excessive pay for CEOs, as well as unabated exploitation of national treasuries, people, and natural resources, are enough indications of this shift. The institutions like the World Bank and IMF, their unfair lending practices, and free trade agreements are acting as catalysts for this paradigm shift (Figure 33).

New World Order: The Rise of Transnational Corporate Republic

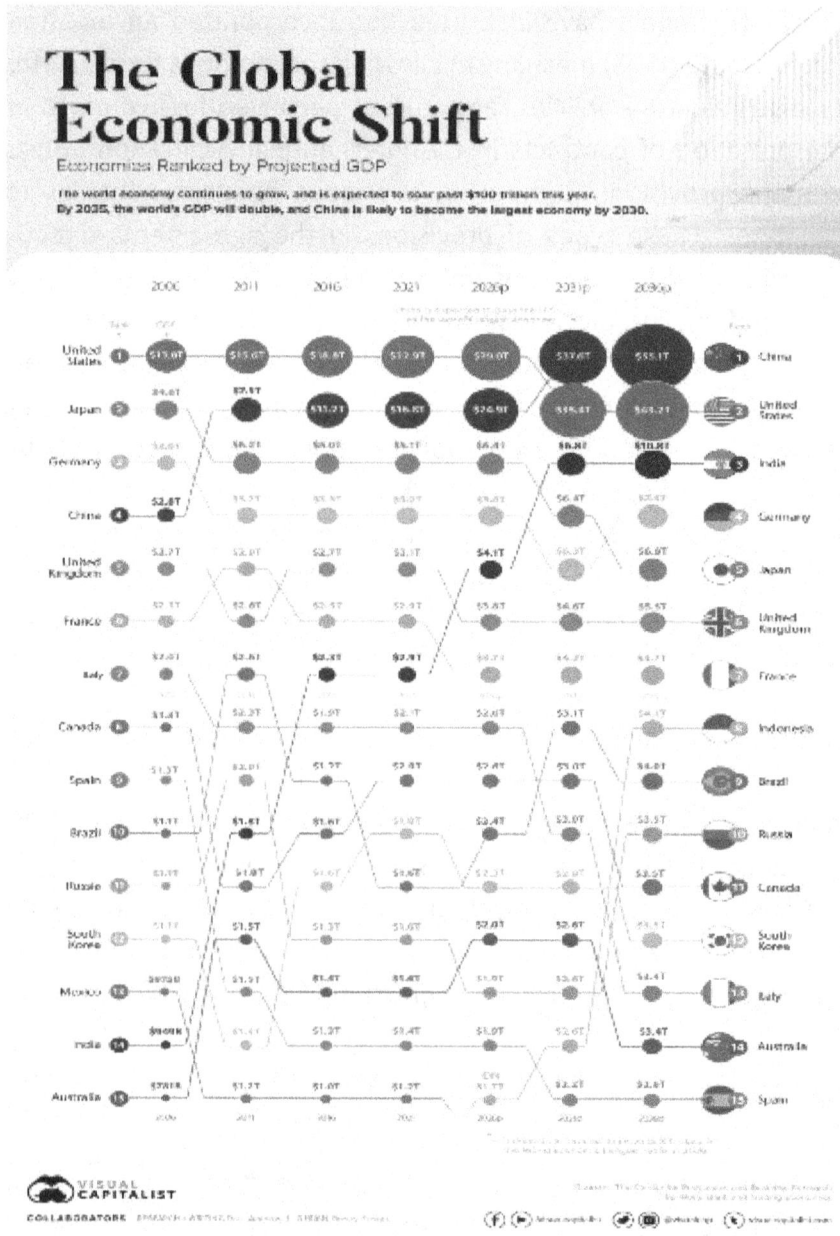

Figure 33: Global Economic Shift;
Source: https://www.visualcapitalist.com/shifting-global-economic-power/

These non-governmental financial institutions are intricately interwoven with government funding systems and have now risen to a position of enormous power over all aspects of global finance (Thorpe, J. D., 2015, February 23).

A corporate republic is an extension of the corporatocracy. A form of government run primarily like a business involving a board of directors and executives, in which all aspects of society are privatised by a single or small group of companies. The ultimate goal of such a state is to increase the wealth of its shareholders.

Utilities, including hospitals (health), schools (education), the military (defence), and the police force (law and order), are likely to be privatised. Social welfare is carried out by corporations in the form of pensions and benefits to employees instead of the state. Globalisation has entered into such a new era in the ongoing evolution of capitalism, distinguished by the development of a globally integrated production and financial system is a characteristic of a typical transnational state.

Besides the economy, the other state organs, like courts, regulatory agencies, executives, and legislatures, are also networking and transgressing daily into and with their counterparts in other nation-states creating a new trans-governmental order. These transnational government networks, including bankers, lawyers, activists, and even criminals, can be seen further in light of the transnational state structure. Global networks of professionals such as accountants and bankers facilitate standardising concepts and practices in different countries. The transnational structural transformations inherent to globalisation have been brought into focus recently and acquired critical importance for the academic and political agenda of the twenty-first century. These changes are transcending the traditional nation-state concept and its relevance.

So far, the globalisation debate has been limited to nation-state economies only. The underlying question is how it will pan out in the new world order. The relationship between globalisation and the nation-state has given rise to an entirely new entity, the transnational state, wherein sometimes the nation-states overlap each other. This process is progressively working towards strengthening the transnational state and relegating the states to irrelevance and rendering them obsolete gradually and eventually. The problem arises because the transnational state and the nation-state are not coterminous. It can be easily deduced that we are amid a tectonic transition from an international to a transnational politico-economic system of a transnational state.

Historically, the East India Company could be described as a prototype of a corporate republic founded by a charter by Elizabeth-I on 31 December 1600. The East India Company was awarded the monopoly to operate and trade in the areas from the Cape of Good Hope on the southern tip of Africa to the Straits of Magellan in South America (Jessen, M. H., 2020, January 30). This company had extensive jurisdiction and rights to have an army, make laws, war or peace, and even have its own mint and flag (Thomson, J.E., 1996). According to Stern (Stern, P.J., 2011), this is nothing less than a corporate state.

Of the Fortune 500 companies on the Forbes list, 119 belong to China, coming second after the US with 121. It is pertinent and vital to ask how some Chinese corporations have become major global players. It must be in the know-how or connivance with the otherwise tightly controlled Chinese government. Rather it is very likely that these corporations may have been picked, promoted and selected by the government as a well-thought-out game plan and strategy to extend Chinese influence and steal foreign technology deliberately (Jones, L., Dr., 2020, August 8).

Some initiatives, like their involvement in nuclear power plants, 5G network building by Huawei and Belt and Road Infrastructure initiative, are worrying, as they should be seen as a part of their grand geopolitical design to trap the developing countries in a debt trap. It is pertinent to note that although the Chinese government has a direct hand in promoting these companies, these companies are allowed to have a free ride to pursue their own profits with very little regulatory pressure, like in the case of the East India Company.

Recently China has found a novel method of sidelining the US dollar and organised with Russia to help it with sidestepping the sanction of the Western countries against Russia in the light of Russian aggression against Ukraine and receive payments for the export of coal from Russia to India in Yuan instead of US dollar, killing two birds in one stone. According to a news report in The Wire, an Indian online news portal UltraTech Cement, the biggest cement producer in India importing a cargo of Russian coal, is paying in Chinese Yuan, an unusual payment method likely to become more common. This deal is said to have been arranged by SUEK from Dubai. Such a trend of using the Yuan to settle payments could help insulate Moscow from the effects of Western sanctions, besides bolstering Beijing's push to internationalise the Yuan currency further and move away from the dominance of the US dollar in global trade.

According to Bill Gates (Gill, B., 2022), China has both capability and intent to position itself at a leveraged geostrategic level against the US and the West ever since the takeover of the CCP by Xi Jinping in 2012. It has adopted a very aggressive and muscular foreign policy to exert itself as a world leader. Its foreign policy initiatives are designed to enhance its legitimacy through respect and appropriation at domestic and international audiences.

This is evident by its assertiveness and claim on disputed territories, like Taiwan, the South and East China Sea and borderlands with India along the Line of Control (LOC).

The Belt and Road Initiative, the Regional Comprehensive Economic Partnership, the Asia Infrastructure Investment Bank, the New

Development Bank, the cooperation between China and the countries of Central and Eastern Europe, the use of its economic might to intimidate, coerce, and buy others to support its interests, as well as its efforts to gain a larger voice in global governance, among other initiatives, have brought China closer to the centre of the global stage.

8 Conclusions

The political institution of democracy and the economic model of capitalism were examined to see how these have undergone a slow and gradual change over time and have evolved their meanings and contexts because of the trepidation and tribulations of the times. These transformations, in conjunction with the rapid advancement of technologies, have played a significant role in changing the behaviour of the institution of democracy and working on the economic modelling of capitalism.

Technological advances, particularly in the field of information technology and telecommunications and the advent of high-speed internet, have extended their overreach and overlap, transgressing the traditional national boundaries and increasing the interconnectivity leading up to interdependent and fast charging the process of globalisation.

Globalisation has then, in turn, affected, changed and furthered the behaviour and nature of sovereign nation-states, thereby creating, promoting and leading to an entirely new and emerging phenomenon in governance, a new concept called corporate governance.

The sovereign nation-states initially provided out-of-the-way special treatment and leverage to the corporations in terms of the allocation of resources and tax concessions. The power and manoeuvrability of these corporations kept growing initially at the national and then at the international level. The power of these corporations grew to such an extent that they then started transgressing into and usurping the powers of the nation-states themselves, at whose behest they got the power.

As a result, the roles of governments and corporations seem to have reversed. Instead of the governments controlling the corporations, the corporations start dictating the terms to the governments to formulate and legislate the policies conducive to the growth of the corporations and furthering their interest. For example, the corporations got hold of the banks and the money supply. These corporations raised their loans from government banks and then got them written off. This has been made easier because of technological advancements that led to the development of a new monetary system of blockchains and cryptocurrency that came in handy to the corporations to tighten their grip on power and governments across the world, demolishing the territorial and monetary sovereignty of any individual country.

As a result, the democracies changed and seamlessly devolved into corporate states as the governments started working as corporations. These state corporations, in turn, further combining democracy with capitalism, gave birth to the next phase of governance known as corporatocracy. While democratic governments were taken over by the corporations elsewhere, the State of China, on the other hand, transformed itself into a corporation and assumed the role of a corporation and became a State Corporation instead of a Corporate State.

By heavily investing in other countries and laying debt traps, it has spread its tentacles far and wide. It has become the Transnational Corporate State Republic, an extension of the corporatocracy, a form of government-run primarily like a business involving a board of directors and executives, in which all aspects of society are privatised by a single or small group of companies.

Notes

Alexandre, A. (2018, October 10). Research: $20 billion raised through ICOS since 2017. *Cointelegraph*. https://cointelegraph.com/news/research-20-billion-raised-through-icos-since-2017

Altman, B. W., & Vidaver-Cohen, D. (2000). A framework for understanding corporate citizenship. *Business and Society Review, 105*(1), 1–7. https://doi.org/10.1111/0045-3609.00061

Amoros, R. (2022, June 13). *Visualising the coming shift in global economic power (2006-2036p)*. Visual Capitalist. https://www.visualcapitalist.com/shifting-global-economic-power/

Anon. (1992, May 1) The decadence of Capitalism. International Communist Current.

Anon. (2012, January 24). *State of power 2012*. Transnational Institute. https://www.tni.org/en/report/state-corporate-power-2012

Anon. (2013, February 17). *A framework for the concept of the decadence of capitalism*. Leftcom. https://www.leftcom.org/en/forum/2013-02-17/a-framework-for-the-concept-of-decadence-of-capitalism

Anon. (2014, May 18). *Analysis of Criminal and Financial background details of Lok Sabha 2014 Winners*. Association for Democratic Reforms. http://adrindia.org/research-and-report/election-watch/lok-sabha/2014/lok-sabha-2014-winners-analysis-criminal-and-finan

Anon. (2019, June 29). *Who owns the media in India?* Media Ownership Monitor. https://india.mom-gmr.org/

Anon. (2021, November 18). *Shell corporations explained: How shell corporations work - 2023*. MasterClass. https://www.masterclass.com/articles/shell-corporation-explained

Anon. (2022, March 1). *Cryptocurrency prices, charts and market capitalisations*. CoinMarketCap. https://coinmarketcap.com/

António, H. O. (2021, June 22). *Global wealth report 2021*. Credit Suisse. https://www.credit-suisse.com/about-us-news/en/articles/media-releases/global-wealth-report-2021-202106.html

Anup, C (2020). The criminalisation of Politics in India. Dissertation Submitted As A Part Of The Master Of Laws In Constitutional And Administrative Law, The National University Of Advanced Legal Studies (Nuals), Kochi, 2020

Aon. (2022, March 1). *Today's top 100 crypto coins prices and data.* CoinMarketCap. https://coinmarketcap.com/coins/

Ashby, H. (2021, January 15). Far-Right extremism is a global problem—and the world needs to come together to address it. *Foreign Policy.* https://foreignpolicy.com/2021/01/15/far-right-extremism-global-problem-worldwide-solutions/

Babic, M., Garcia-Bernardo, J., & Heemskerk, E. M. (2019). The rise of transnational state capital: State-led foreign investment in the 21st century. *Review of International Political Economy, 27*(3), 433–475. https://doi.org/10.1080/09692290.2019.1665084

Bajpai, P. P. (2022). Modi's new policy: किसी सरकार ने ऐसा काम कभी नहीं किया... [Video]. In *YouTube.* https://www.youtube.com/watch?v=1FLvDGj0ZLU.

Barbier, C. L. (2017, October 14). *Corporatocracy and capitalism.* Christophe L Barbier - Academia.Edu. https://www.academia.edu/34858106/Corporatocracy_and_Capitalism

Bauman, Z. (1998). Globalisation: The Human Consequences. United Kingdom: Columbia University Press.

Bergin, T. (2020, May 28). Exclusive: U.S. taxpayers' virus relief went to firms that avoided U.S. taxes. *Reuters.* https://www.reuters.com/article/us-health-coronavirus-companies-tax-excl-idUSKBN2341ZE

Bhandari, R. (2013, March 1). Rise of the global corporatocracy: An interview with John Perkins. *Monthly Review.* https://monthlyreview.org/2013/03/01/rise-of-the-global-corporatocracy-an-interview-with-john-perkins/

Bickerton, C., & Accetti, C. I. (2015). Populism and technocracy: Opposites or complements? *Critical Review of International Social and Political Philosophy, 20*(2), 186–206. https://doi.org/10.1080/13698230.2014.995504

Bieler, A., & Morton, A.D. (2011). The will-o'-the-wisp of the transnational state. *Journal of Australian Political Economy, 23.*

Blatter, J., & Schulz, J. (2022). Intergovernmentalism and the crisis of representative democracy: The case for creating a system of horizontally expanded and overlapping national democracies. European Journal of International Relations, 28(3), 722–747. https://doi.org/10.1177/13540661221106909

Boar, C., & Wehrli, A. (2021, January 27). *Ready, steady, go?* Results of the Third BIS Survey on Central Bank Digital Currency. https://www.bis.org/publ/bppdf/bispap114.htm

Brown, D. L. (2012). Roger Coate and Markus Thiel (eds)Identity Politics in the Age of Globalization Boulder, CO: Lynne Rienner, 2010, 207 pp.$65.00 hbk. *Studies in Ethnicity and Nationalism, 12*(3), 550–551. https://doi.org/10.1111/sena.12003

Brunnermeier, M. K., James, H., & Landau, J. P. (2021). The digitisation of money (BIS working papers' no. 941). https://www.bis.org/publ/work941.htm

Campion, K., & Poynting, S. (2021). International nets and national links: The global rise of the extreme right—introduction to special issues. *Social Sciences*, *10*(2), 61. https://doi.org/10.3390/socsci10020061

Caponnetto, M. (2023, January 3). *Debt system and capitalism: What are the links?* – CADTM. CADTM. https://www.cadtm.org/Debt-system-and-capitalism-what

Carroll, A. B. (1998). The four faces of corporate citizenship. *Business and Society Review*, *100–101*(1), 1–7. https://doi.org/10.1111/0045-3609.00008

Carter, E. (2018). Right-wing extremism/radicalism: Reconstructing the concept. *Journal of Political Ideologies*, *23*(2), 157–182. https://doi.org/10.1080/13569317.2018.1451227

Castells, M. (2004). The Information Age: Economy. Society and Culture-End of Millenium, Oxford: Blackwell

Chengu, G. (2013, December 19). Capitalism: A cancer that threatens civilisation. *The Chronicle*. https://www.chronicle.co.zw/capitalism-a-cancer-that-threatens-civilisation/

Choyleva, D. (2021, July 1). China advances in challenge to dollar hegemony. Financial Times. https://www.ft.com/content/efa3ec2b-5be8-413f-b23c-cc9b9bff1261

Chubb, A. (2022). The securitisation of 'Chinese influence' in Australia. *Journal of Contemporary China*, *32*(139), 17–34. https://doi.org/10.1080/10670564.2022.2052437

Daniali, H., & Flaten, M. A. (2021). Experiencing COVID-19 symptoms without the disease: The role of nocebo in reporting symptoms. *Scandinavian Journal of Public Health*, *50*(1), 61–69. https://doi.org/10.1177/14034948211018385

de Caria, R. (2019). Blockchain-Based money as the ultimate challenge to sovereignty. *European Journal of Comparative Law and Governance*, *6*(2), 131–145. https://doi.org/10.1163/22134514-00602004

Desai, M., & Dharmapala, D. (2009). Corporate tax avoidance and firm value, Vol 91, No 3 (pp. 357–547). The Review of Economics and Statistics.

Desai, S. (2022, May 26). Fake News," Lies and Propaganda: How to Sort Fact from Fiction: Research Guides at the University of Michigan Library. https://guides.lib.umich.edu/fakenews

Desjardins, J. (2022, July 7). *The evolution of media: Visualising a data-driven future* Visual Capitalist. https://www.visualcapitalist.com/evolution-of-media-data-future/

Dixon, A. D., & Monk, A. H. B. (2011). Rethinking the sovereign in sovereign wealth funds. Transactions of the Institute of British Geographers, 37 (1), 104–117.

Doan, P. (2016, April 30). The United States Corporatocracy and its Imperialist Agenda to Achieve Full Spectrum Dominance. Phil Doan - Academia.Edu.

https://www.academia.edu/24906416/The_United_States_Corporatocracy_and_its_Imperialist_Agenda_to_Achieve_Full_Spectrum_Dominance

Duraisamy, P., & Jérôme, B. (2017). Who wins the Indian parliament election: Criminals, the wealthy and incumbents? *Journal of Social and Economic Development, 19*(2), 245–262. https://doi.org/10.1007/s40847-017-0044-0

Enfield, N. (2019). Ideas and tactics for making it through the post-truth maze. The University of Sydney. https://www.sydney.edu.au/research/research-impact/ideas-and-tactics-for-making-it-through-the-post-truth-maze.html

Erman, E., & Uhlin, A. (2010). *Legitimacy beyond the state?* Palgrave Mcmillan. https://link.springer.com/book/10.1057/9780230283251 (Original work published 2010)

Fuchs, D., Kalfagianni, A., Sattelberger, J. (2010). Democratic Legitimacy of Transnational Corporations in Global Governance. In: Erman, E., Uhlin, A. (eds)

Funnell, B. (2009, July 1). Debt is Capitalism's dirty little Secret. Financial Times. https://www.ft.com/content/e23c6d04-659d-11de-8e34-00144feabdc0

Garza, A. (2019, September 24). *Identity politics: Friend or foe?* Othering & Belonging Institute. https://belonging.berkeley.edu/identity-politics-friend-or-foe

Georgescu, P. (2021, July 21). The shareholders are not the owners of A corporation. *Forbes.* https://www.forbes.com/sites/petergeorgescu/2021/07/21/the-shareholders-are-not-the-owners-of-a-corporation/?sh=337146b31e0a

Georgieva, Kristalina. (2022, February 10). The future of money: Gearing up for central bank digital currency. MercoPress. https://en.mercopress.com/2022/02/10/the-future-of-money-gearing-up-for-central-bank-digital-currency?fr=operanews

Gill, B. (2022). *Daring to struggle: China's global ambitions under Xi Jinping*. Oxford University Press.

Gleckman, H. (2019, July 3). The UN signs a deal with Davos that threatens democratic principles. Transnational Institute. https://www.tni.org/en/article/un-signs-deal-with-davos-that-threatens-democratic-principles

Graham, A., & Davies, G. (1997). *Broadcasting, society and policy in the multimedia age.* University of Luton Press.

Gross, M. (2017). The dangers of a post-truth world. *Current Biology, 27*(1), R1–R4. https://doi.org/10.1016/j.cub.2016.12.034

Guibernau, M. (2010). Migration and the rise of the radical right. Social Malaise and the Failure of Mainstream Politics. Retrieved March 8, 2016, from http://www.policy-network.net/publications_download.aspx?ID = 3684

Hallin, D., & Mancini, P. (2004). Comparing media systems. Three models of media and politics. Cambridge, UK: Cambridge University Press.

Hanna, T. (2019, August 24). *Buyouts, not bailouts: Public banks as a solution to the next crisis.* OpenDemocracy. https://www.opendemocracy.net/en/oureconomy/buyouts-not-bailouts-public-banks-solution-next-crisis/

Hanton, A. (2012, January 16). Top 10 disadvantages to capitalism. *Listverse.Com* https://listverse.com/2012/01/16/top-10-disadvantages-to-capitalism/

Harrison, S., & Bruter, M. (2011). Mapping extreme right ideology. Empirical geography of the European extreme right. London: Palgrave Macmillan

Heemskerk, E. (2018, July 10). *Who is more powerful – states or corporations?* The Conversation. https://theconversation.com/who-is-more-powerful-states-or-corporations-99616

Heffer, S. (2021, August 31). *Identity politics: The threat to society*. The Centre for Independent Studies. https://www.cis.org.au/publication/the-threat-of-identity-politics/

Herman, E., & McChesney, R. (1997). The global media. New missionaries of global capitalism. London: Cassell.

Huang, Y., & Mayer, M. (2022). Digital currencies, monetary sovereignty, and U.S.–China power competition. Policy & Internet, 14(2), 324–347. https://doi.org/10.1002/poi3.302

Ignazi, P. (1992). The silent counter-revolution. Hypotheses on the emergence of extreme right-wing parties in Europe. European Journal of Political Research, 22(1), 3–34

Jaffrelot, C., & Verniers, G. (2020). The BJP's 2019 election campaign: Not business as usual. *Contemporary South Asia, 28*(2), 155–177. https://doi.org/10.1080/09584935.2020.1765985

Jalan, A., & Vaidyanathan, R. (2017). Tax havens Conduit for corporate tax malfeasance. *Journal of Financial Regulation and Compliance, 25*(1), 86–104. https://doi.org/10.1108/JFRC-04-2016-0039

Jessen, M. H. (2020, January 30). The corporate state. Transnational Institute. https://www.tni.org/en/publication/the-corporate-state

Jones, L., Dr. (2020, August 8). Beyond China, Inc: Understanding Chinese companies. Longreads. https://longreads.tni.org/stateofpower/understanding-chinese-companies-beyond-china-inc

Karolyi, G. A., & Liao, R. C. (2017). State capitalism's global reach: Evidence from foreign acquisitions by state-owned companies. Journal of Corporate Finance, 42, 367–391.

Kitty, J. (2013, December 6). *The coming Corporatocracy and the death of democracy*. Politics and Insights. https://politicsandinsights.org/2013/12/06/the-coming-corporatocracy-and-the-death-of-democracy/.

Klein, N. (2014). *The shock doctrine: The rise of disaster capitalism*. Penguin UK.

Köhler, D., & Ebner, J. (2019). Strategies and tactics: communication strategies of jihadists and right-wing extremists. In *Hate Speech and Radicalisation Online The OCCI Research Report*

Kshetri, N., & Voas, J. (2017a). The economics of "fake news." *IT Professional, 19*(6), 8–12. https://doi.org/10.1109/mitp.2017.4241459

Kuyper, J. W. (2018). Democratic legitimacy beyond the state: Politicisation, representation, and a systemic framework. *Moral Philosophy and Politics,* 5(2), 281–303. https://doi.org/10.1515/mopp-2018-0014

Lai, K. P. Y., Lin, S., & Sidaway, J. D. (2020). Financing the Belt and Road Initiative (BRI): Research agendas beyond the "debt-trap" discourse. *Eurasian Geography and Economics, 61*(2), 109–124. https://doi.org/10.1080/15387216.2020.1726787

Lane, D. (2009). Global capitalism and the transformation of state socialism. *Studies in Comparative International Development, 44*(2), 97–117. https://doi.org/10.1007/s12116-008-9039-3

Langenmayr, D., & Zyska, L. (2021). Escaping the Exchange of Information: Tax Evasion Via Citizenship-by-Investment (2021). CESifo Working Paper No. 8956, Available at SSRN: https://ssrn.com/abstract=3812073 or http://dx.doi.org/10.2139/ssrn.3812073

Liu, H., & Lim, G. (2022). When the state goes transnational: The political economy of China's engagement with Indonesia. *Competition & Change,* 0(0). https://doi.org/10.1177/10245294221103069

Mahurkar, U., & Punj, S. (2018, May 10). Uday Mahurkar. India Today. https://www.indiatoday.in/magazine/the-big-story/story/20180521-india-public-sector-bank-npa-vijay-mallya-nirav-modi-debt-bailout-1231739-2018-05-10

Marsden, C.T. (2000). The New Corporate Citizenship of Big Business: Part of the Solution to Sustainability? *Business and Society Review, 105,* 8-25.

Martin, N., & Picherit, D. (2019). Special issue: Electoral fraud and manipulation in India and Pakistan. *Commonwealth & Comparative Politics, 58*(1), 1–20. https://doi.org/10.1080/14662043.2020.1700016

Matten, D., and A. Crane (2005) 'Corporate Citizenship: Toward an Extended Theoretical Conceptualisation', Academy of Management Review 30.1: 166-79.

McGoey, S. (2021, November 19). *Nearly $500 billion is lost yearly to global tax abuse due mostly to corporations, a new analysis says - ICIJ.* International Consortium of Investigative Journalists. https://www.icij.org/inside-icij/2021/11/nearly-500-billion-lost-yearly-to-global-tax-abuse-due-mostly-to-corporations-new-analysis-says

McIntyre, L. (2018c). Post-Truth. MIT Press.

Menczer, F. (2020b, December 1). Information overload helps fake news spread, and social media knows it. Scientific American. https://www.scientificamerican.com/article/information-overload-helps-fake-news-spread-and-social-media-knows-it/

Miraz, M. H., & Ali, M. (2019, January 31). *Applications of blockchain technology beyond cryptocurrency.* SSRN Papers. https://papers.ssrn.com/sol3/papers.cfm?abstract_id=3318926

Mirchandani, M. (2018, August 29). Digital hatred, real violence: Majoritarian radicalisation and social media in India. *Observational Research Foundation.*

https://www.orfonline.org/research/43665-digital-hatred-real-violence-majoritarian-radicalisation-and-social-media-in-india/

Mitra, S., Mitra, A., & Mukherji, A. (2016, January 1). *Cash for votes: Evidence from India on election financing and dynastic politics*. IIMB-. https://repository.iimb.ac.in/handle/2074/14609

Mudde, C. (2002). *The ideology of the extreme right*. New York, NY: Manchester University Press.

Murali, A.G.A.C.I.V.S. (2017, November 30). *Sam Dastyari and the Chinese government's influence in Australia*. Lowy Institute. https://www.lowyinstitute.org/the-interpreter/sam-dastyari-chinese-government-influence-australia

Murphy, R. (2008, June 30). *Tax Havens Creating Turmoil: The Tax Justice Network submission to the Treasury Select Committee*. Tax Research UK. https://www.taxresearch.org.uk/Blog/2008/06/30/tax-havens-creating-turmoil-the-tax-justice-network-submission-to-the-treasury-select-committee/

Mystakidis, S. (2022). Metaverse. *Encyclopedia*, 2(1), 486–497. https://doi.org/10.3390/encyclopedia2010031

News, B. (2022, February 16). *UK scraps rich foreign investor visa scheme*. BBC News. https://www.bbc.com/news/uk-politics-60410844

Northcott, M. S. (1993b). New world order or new world enemies? *New Blackfriars*, 74(872), 316–327. https://doi.org/10.2307/43249463

Oliver, T. (2018, June 26). *Here's a better way to think about identity politics*. The Conversation. https://theconversation.com/heres-a-better-way-to-think-about-identity-politics-84144

Pavlidis, G. (2021). A case of insufficient safeguards or state-enabled money laundering? 'Golden Passport' and 'Golden Visa' investment schemes in Europe. *Journal of Investment Compliance*, 22(2), 170–179. https://doi.org/10.1108/joic-01-2021-0002

Pejovich, S. (1990, January 1). *The rise of capitalism*. Springer Netherlands. https://link.springer.com/chapter/10.1007/978-0-585-28557-3_2

Perkins, J. (2004a). Confessions of an economic hitman. Berrett-Koehler Publishers

Plimer, I. (2009). *Heaven and earth: Global warming: The missing science*. Connor Court.

Pogonyi, S. (2011). Dual citizenship and sovereignty. *Nationalities Papers*, 39(5), 685–704. https://doi.org/10.1080/00905992.2011.599377

Prakash, A. (2019, April 12). The dynamics of social media and the Indian Elections 2019. Asia Dialogue.

Raveendran, K. (2022, April 7). *Lanka victim of Chinese debt trap diplomacy*. The Meghalayan. https://themeghalayan.com/lanka-victim-of-chinese-debt-trap-diplomacy/

Redman, J. (2017, October 31). *Satoshi Nakamoto's brilliant white paper turns 9-years old – technology bitcoin news*. Bitcoin News. https://news.bitcoin.com/satoshi-nakamotos-brilliant-white-paper-turns-9-years-old/

Reiff, N. (2022, July 13). How much of all money is in bitcoin? *Investopedia*. https://www.investopedia.com/tech/how-much-worlds-money-bitcoin/

Rickards, J. (2014). *The death of money: The coming collapse of the international monetary system*. Penguin.

Rivas, T. (2020, October 18). *Corporatocracy: A Global Empire Introduction The corporatocracy represents more than a group of individuals focused on*. Course Hero. https://www.coursehero.com/file/70822112/Thomas-Rpdf/.

Robinson, W. I., & Harris, J. (2000). Towards a Global Ruling Class? Globalisation and the Transnational Capitalist Class. *Science & Society, 64*(1), 11–54. http://www.jstor.org/stable/40403824

Rose, C. (2015). The evolution of digital currencies: Bitcoin, a cryptocurrency causing a monetary revolution. International Business & Economics Research Journal, 14(4), 617–621.

Rosen, P. (2022, June 27). China is building a yuan currency reserve to compete with the dollar and prop up other economies facing volatility. *Markets Insider*. https://markets.businessinsider.com/news/currencies/dollar-vs-yuan-china-currency-reserve-to-combat-us-2022-6?amp

Routley, N. (2022, June 29). *33 problems with media in one chart*. Visual Capitalist. https://www.visualcapitalist.com/problems-with-media/

Sandhar, H.(2022). Kisan Nama: Farmer's Odyssey. Harkirat Singh Sandhar

Schaik, L. G. V., & de Pas, R. van. (2014, July 15). Transnational Governance and Democratic Legitimacy: The case of Global Health. Unknown. http://dx.doi.org/10.13140/RG.2.1.2070.5120

Schelling, C. (2019, May 21). The problem with capitalism? We don't have enough of it. *Institutional Investor*. https://www.institutionalinvestor.com/article/b1fhs3c4bs1mh8/The-Problem-With-Capitalism-We-Don-t-Have-Enough-of-It

Seitz, B. (2002). The economic approach to corporate citizenship: The economic argument. In H. von Weltzien Hoivik (Ed.), Moral leadership in action: 42–52. Cheltenham, UK: Edward Elgar.

Shaw, H. J. (2008). The Rise of Corporatocracy in a Disenchanted Age. Human Geography, 1(1), 1–11. https://doi.org/10.1177/194277860800100113

Shen, D. (2012). The public sphere: Journal of public policy. *The Public Sphere: Journal of Public Policy, 1*(1).

Shmargad, Y., & Sanchez, L. (2020). Social media influence and electoral competition. Social Science Computer Review, 40(1), 4–23.

Sidhu, A. (2020, April 6). A different contagion: India's bank bailouts. Geopolitical Monitor. https://www.geopoliticalmonitor.com/a-different-contagion-indias-bank-bailouts

Skypala, P. (2009, September 8). Tackling 'ownerless' corporations. Financial Times. https://www.ft.com/content/957fdd9c-cb06-11de-97e0-00144feabdc0

Sommerlad, N. (2013, March 23). *Who really won the Iraq war? Oil barons, big business and mercenaries* Mirror. https://www.mirror.co.uk/news/world-news/iraq-war-winners-were-oil-1779740

Stern, P.J. (2011) The Company-State. Corporate Sovereignty and the Early Modern Foundations of the British Empire in India. Oxford & New York: Oxford University Press.

Sumption, Jonathan. (2021). Law in a time of crisis. Allen & Unwin.

Tanenhaus, S. (2011). Whittaker Chambers: A Biography. United Kingdom: Random House Publishing Group.

Thomson, J.E. (1996) Mercenaries, Pirates, and Sovereigns: State-Building and Extraterritorial Violence in Early Modern Europe. Princeton studies international history and politics. Princeton, NJ: Princeton University Press, p. 32–35.

Thorpe, J. D. (2015, February 23). *Do corporations rule the world?* John D Thorpe - Academia.Edu. https://www.academia.edu/11017677/Do_Corporations_Rule_the_World

Vaishnav, M. (2017, January 24). *When crime pays: Money and muscle in Indian politics*. Carnegie Endowment for International Peace. https://carnegieendowment.org/2017/01/24/when-crime-pays-money-and-muscle-in-indian-politics-pub-66205

Vaishnav, M. (2019, November 25). *Electoral bonds: The safeguards of Indian democracy are crumbling*. Carnegie Endowment for International Peace. https://carnegieendowment.org/2019/11/25/electoral-bonds-safeguards-of-indian-democracy-are-crumbling-pub-80428

Van Staden, C., Alden, C., & Wu, Y.-S. (2018). In the driver's seat? African agency and Chinese power at FOCAC, the AU and the BRI (Occasional Paper No. 286). Retrieved from https://saiia.org.za/research/in-the-drivers-seat-african-agency-and-chinese-power/

Vattamattam, S. (2020a, February 21). *Post-truth and the return of fascism* Sebastian Vattamattam - Academia.Edu. https://www.academia.edu/42036340/Post_truth_and_the_Return_of_Fascism

Waldek, L., & Droogan, J. (2021, August 16). Right-wing extremism weaponises democracy against itself. The Sydney Morning Herald.

West, M. (2017, February 20). *Australia's march towards corporatocracy*. The Conversation. https://theconversation.com/australias-march-towards-corporatocracy-73192

Wiist, W. (2011, July). Citizens United, public health, and democracy: The Supreme Court's ruling, implications, and proposed action. American Journal of Public Health,7, 1172-1179. doi:10.2105/AJPH.2010.300043

Williams, M. T. (2014, February 14). Finance professor: Bitcoin could evolve into an existential threat worthy of a science fiction movie. Insider. https://www.businessinsider.com/bitcoin-sovereign-attack-2014-2

Zattoni, A. (2011). Who should control a corporation? Toward a contingency stakeholder model for allocating ownership rights. *Journal of Business Ethics*, *103*(2), 255–274. https://doi.org/10.1007/s10551-011-0864-3

Bibliography

Acharya, A. (2000). Developing countries and the emerging world order: Security and Institutions. In L. Fawcett & Y. Sayigh (Eds.), The Third World Beyond the Cold War: Continuity and Change (pp. 78–98). Oxford University PressOxford. http://dx.doi.org/10.1093/0198295510.003.0005

ADR. (2022, April 11). Electoral Bonds And Opacity In Political Funding.

Agnew, J., (1994), 'Global Hegemony versus National Economy. The United States in the New World Order, in Demko, G., Wood, W. (eds), Re-Ordering the World. Oxford: Westview Press, 269–279.

Aidt, T., Asatryan, Z., Badalyan, L. and F. Heinemann. (2020). 'Vote Buying or (Political) Business (Cycles) as Usual?' The Review of Economics and Statistics, 2020 102:3, 409-425.

Aidt T, Golden M, Tiwari D (2011) Incumbents and criminals in the Indian national legislature. Working paper version 5.0, Department of Political Science, University of California-Los Angeles

Akinci, G., & Crittle, J. (2008). Special economic zone: performance, lessons learned, and implication for zone development. Washington DC: World Bank, 2008, pp. 9–11

Albert, M., (1992), 'Conspiracy Theory', Z Magazine, May. (http://zena.secureforum.com/Znet/zmag/zarticle.cfm?Url=articles/oldalbert19.htm).

Alison Millington - Business Insider. (2019, January 2). 23 countries where money can buy you a second passport or "elite residency." Evening Standard. https://www.standard.co.uk/escapist/travel/countries-where-money-can-buy-you-a-second-passport-or-residency-a4028361.html

Amoros, R. (2022a, February 1). Visualising the state of global debt by country. Visual Capitalist. https://www.visualcapitalist.com/global-debt-to-gdp-ratio/

Anon, (2012) 'State of Power.' Transnational Institute, 24 Jan. 2012, https://www.tni.org/en/report/state-corporate-power-2012.

Anon, (2021, Feb 9) State of Power, Transnational Institute. www.tni.org/en/report/state-corporate-power-2012.

Anon. (2014). Bhutan's gross national happiness index. OPHI. https://ophi.org.uk/policy/gross-national-happiness-index/

Bibliography

Anon. (2020, September 9). Pandemic profits for companies soar by billions more as the poorest pay the price. Oxfam International.

Anon. (2021, June 19). Insights into Editorial: Needed: Full disclosure on electoral bonds. Insightsias.

Anon (2014) Media Control and Ownership Policy Background Paper No.3. Department of Infrastructure, Transport, Regional Development, Communications and the Arts, 2014, https://www.infrastructure.gov.au/department/media/publications/media-control-and-ownership-policy-background-paper-no3.

Ashish. (2018, Feb 12) 'If All Large Countries Are In Debt, Who Do They Borrow Money From?' ScienceABC.

Babic, M., Fichtner, J., & Heemskerk, E. M. (2017). States versus corporations: Rethinking the power of business in international politics. The International Spectator, 52(4), 20–43. https://doi.org/10.1080/03932729.2017.1389151

Barrett, P., Das, S., & Magistretti, G. (2021, July 30). After-Effects of the COVID-19 pandemic: Prospects for medium-term economic damage. IMF. https://www.imf.org/en/Publications/WP/Issues/2021/07/30/After-Effects-of-the-COVID-19-Pandemic-Prospects-for-Medium-Term-Economic-Damage-462898

Bebchuk, L. A. (2003). The case for increasing shareholder power. SSRN Electronic Journal. https://doi.org/10.2139/ssrn.631344

Bernstein, M. (2005). Identity politics. Annual Review of Sociology, 31, 47–74. https://doi.org/10.2307/29737711

Bhattacharjee, A., Wang, L., & Banerjee, T. (2016). Media ownership and concentration in India. In Who Owns the World's Media? (pp. 772–800). Oxford University Press. http://dx.doi.org/10.1093/acprof:oso/9780199987238.003.0025

Bock, & Fuccillo. (1975). Transnational corporations as international political actors. Studies in Comparative International Development, 10(2), 51–77. https://doi.org/10.1007/BF02800444

Boon, A. (2022). Corporatocracy. In Lawyers and the Rule of Law. Hart Publishing. http://dx.doi.org/10.5040/9781509925247.ch-015

Brennan, B., and Gonzalo Berrón. (2020, January 14). The growth of corporate power and the decline of the public interest. Brewminate: A Bold Blend of News and Ideas. https://brewminate.com/the-growth-of-corporate-power-and-the-decline-of-the-public-interest/

Bresheeth, H. (1991). The new world order. The Gulf War and the New World Order (pp.243-256), Zed Books, Editors: Haim Bresheeth and Nira Yuval-Davis

Brierly, J. L. (1963). The Law of Nations: An introduction to the international law of peace. Oxford University Press.

Brunnermeier, M. K., James, H., & Landau, J.- P. (2021). The digitisation of money (BIS working papers' no. 941). https://www.bis.org/publ/work941.htm

Brzezinski, Z. (2016). The Grand Chessboard: American Primacy and Its Geostrategic Imperatives. Hachette UK.

Carroll, W. K., & Carson, C. (2003). Forging a new hegemony? The role of transnational policy groups in the network and discourses of global corporate governance. *Journal of World-Systems Research, 9*(1), 67–102. https://doi.org/10.5195/jwsr.2003.257

Centola, D. (2020, Oct 15). Why Social Media Makes Us More Polarised and How to Fix It. Scientific American.

Chengu, G. (2013, December 19). Capitalism: Cancer that threatens civilisation. The Chronicle. https://www.chronicle.co.zw/capitalism-a-cancer-that-threatens-civilisation/

Chomsky, N., & Waterstone, M. (2021). Consequences of capitalism: Manufacturing discontent and resistance. Penguin UK.

Coate, R. A., & Thiel, M. (2010). Identity politics in the age of globalisation. First Forum Press.

Cooper, M. N. (2003). Media ownership and democracy in the digital information age: Promoting diversity with first amendment principles and market structure analysis. Consumer Federation of Amer.

Critchley, P., (1995). Transnational Corporate Capitalism. [e-book] Available through: Academia website <http://mmu.academia.edu/PeterCritchley/Papers

Dalby, Simon, et al. (2003), The Geopolitics Reader. Routledge

Dalio, R. (2021). Changing world order: Why nations succeed or fail. Simon & Schuster.

DeBoom, M.J. (2020). Who is afraid of 'debt-trap diplomacy'? Geopolitical narratives, agency and the multiscalar distribution of risk. Area Development and Policy, 5, 15 - 22.

de Jouvenel, B. (2012). Sovereignty: An Inquiry Into the Political Good. United Kingdom: Cambridge University Press.

Dent, C. M. (2003). Transnational capital, the state and foreign economic policy: Singapore, South Korea and Taiwan. Review of International Political Economy, 10(2), 246–277. https://doi.org/10.2307/4177460

Dice, M. (2010). The new world order: Facts & fiction. Mark Dice

Dimin, L. S. (2011). Corporatocracy: A Revolution in Progress. United States: iUniverse.

Dixon, M. (1982). Dual power: The rise of the transnational corporation and the nation-state: Conceptual explanations to meet popular demand. Contemporary Marxism, 5, 129–146. https://doi.org/10.2307/29765709

Dube, R. (2020, September 21). GDP vs GNH: Rethinking what A healthy economy means. Forbes. https://www.forbes.com/sites/robdube/2020/09/21/gdp-vs-gnh-rethinking-what-a-healthy-economy-means/?sh=74d3f60055df

Bibliography

Duffy, M. (2002). "Shareholder democracy or shareholder plutocracy? Corporate governance and the plight of small shareholders' ' 28; (2002) 25(2) UNSW law journal 434. http://classic.austlii.edu.au/au/journals/UNSWLawJl/2002/28.html

Duraisamy, P., & Jérôme, B. (2017b). Who wins the Indian parliament election: Criminals, the wealthy and incumbents? Journal of Social and Economic Development, 19(2), 245–262. https://doi.org/10.1007/s40847-017-0044-0

Erve, M. V. D. (2006). The Future of Society. The Future of Society.

Faccio, M., Masulis, R. W., & McCONNELL, J. J. (2006). Political connections and corporate bailouts. The Journal of Finance, 61(6), 2597–2635. https://doi.org/10.1111/j.1540-6261.2006.01000.x

F H. Hinsley, Sovereignty (1966); A. James, Sovereign Statehood (1986)

Galbraith, J. K. (2004). The economics of innocent fraud. Penguin Canada.

Gangte, L. (2020, April 1). The debt-trap diplomacy revisited: A case study on Sri Lanka's Hambantota port. Christ University Bangalore - Artha Journal of Social Sciences. https://www.researchgate.net/publication/347586679_The_Debt-Trap_Diplomacy_Revisited_A_Case_Study_on_Sri_Lanka's_Hambantota_Port

Garcia-Bernardo, J., Janský, P., & Tørsløv, T. (2021). Multinational corporations and tax havens: Evidence from country-by-country reporting. International Tax and Public Finance, 28(6), 1519–1561. https://doi.org/10.1007/s10797-020-09639-w

Gneiting, U., Lusiani, Nicholas, & Tamir, I. (2022, May 25). Power, profits and the pandemic. Oxfam International.

Goey, F. de. (2014). Perspectives on European Economic and Social History - Perspektiven der Europäischen Wirtschafts- und Sozialgeschichte. Nomos Verlagsgesellschaft mbH & Co. KG. http://dx.doi.org/10.5771/9783845242590

Goldstein, Judith L.; Rivers, Douglas; Tomz, Michael (2007). "Institutions in International Relations: Understanding the Effects of the GATT and the WTO on World Trade". International Organisation. 61 (1): 37–67.

Graphics, R. (2019, May 25). Drugs, gold, cash and alcohol. Reuters.

Gupta, Manav, (2018) Blockchain for Dummies, John Wiley & Sons, Inc

Gupta, U. (2021, March 10). The Grand Chessboard: American Primacy And Its Geostrategic Imperatives: Brzezinski, Zbigniew: 9780465027262: Books. Amazon.

Hanna, T. (2019, August 28). Buyouts, not bailouts: Public banks as a solution to the next crisis. OpenDemocracy. https://www.opendemocracy.net/en/oureconomy/buyouts-not-bailouts-public-banks-solution-next-crisis/

Hanton, A. (2012, January 16). Top 10 disadvantages to capitalism. Listverse.Com. https://listverse.com/2012/01/16/top-10-disadvantages-to-capitalism/

Hayes, A. (2022, December 30). Corporate citizenship: What it means, 5 stages, and examples. Investopedia. https://www.investopedia.com/terms/c/corporatecitizenship.asp

Heyes, C. (2008). Identity politics. PhilPapers. https://philpapers.org/rec/HEYIP

Hinsley, F. H. (1986). Sovereignty. CUP Archive.

Hoffman, S. G. (2018). The responsibilities and obligations of STS in a moment of post-truth demagoguery. Engaging Science, Technology, and Society, 4, 444–452. https://doi.org/10.17351/ests2018.259

Horsman, Marshall (1994), After the Nation-State: Citizens, Tribalism and the New World Disorder. London: Harper Collins.

https://doi.org/10.4324/9781351034661

Ilias Alami, Adam D. Dixon, Emma Mawdsley. (2021) State Capitalism and the New Global D/development Regime. Antipode 53:5, pages 1294-1318.

Ilias Alami, Adam D. Dixon. (2022) 'Expropriation of Capitalist by State Capitalist:' Organisational Change and the Centralisation of Capital as State Property. Economic Geography 0:0 pages 1-24.

Ilias Alami, Milan Babic, Adam D. Dixon, Imogen T. Liu. (2022) Special issue introduction: what is the new state capitalism?. Contemporary Politics 0:0, pages 1-19

Jakobeit, L, (2011). Transnational Corporations as Political Actors. GRIN Verlag.

James, A. (1986). Sovereign statehood: The basis of international society. Unwin Hyman.

James, A. (1999). The practice of sovereign statehood in contemporary international society. Political Studies, 47(3), 457–473. https://doi.org/10.1111/1467-9248.00212

Jones, M. T., & Haigh, M. (2007). The transnational corporation and new corporate citizenship theory. Journal of Corporate Citizenship, 2007(27), 51–69. https://doi.org/10.9774/gleaf.4700.2007.au.00007

Josh Rosenau, (2008, September 24), Evolution, climate change, plate tectonics, and string theory National Centre for Science Education Columbia University Press

Kato, T. (2005). Challenges to the international monetary system: Rebalancing currencies, institutions, and rates. IMF. https://www.imf.org/en/News/Articles/2015/09/28/04/53/sp093007

Khalil, L. (2022, August 30). Rise of the Extreme Right: A Lowy institute paper: Penguin special by Lydia Khalil. Penguin Books Australia. https://www.penguin.com.au/books/rise-of-the-extreme-right-a-lowy-institute-paper-penguin-special-9781761046353

Kinder, M., Bach, K., & Stateler, L. (2022, April 21). Profits and the pandemic: As shareholder wealth soared, workers were left behind. Brookings.

Kobrin, S. J., Scherer, A. G., & Palazzo, G. (2008). 12 Globalisation, transnational corporations and the future of global governance. Handbook of Research on Global Corporate Citizenship, Edward Elgar, Cheltenham, 249-272.

Korten, D. (2015). "When Corporations Rule The World by David C. Korten." Penguin Books Australia, 2015, https://www.penguin.com.au/books/when-corporations-rule-the-world-9781626562875.

Bibliography

Kovalenko, M., Ziuz, D., Shimunova, O., Bondar, N., & Omelchenko, H. (2020). Implementation of state economic policy under corporatocracy: Financial and credit aspect. Public Policy And Administration, 19(3), 36–47. https://doi.org/10.5755/j01.ppaa.19.3.26842

Kovalenko, M., Ziuz, D., Smihunova, O., Bondar, N., & Omelchenko, H. (2020). Implementation of state economic policy under corporatocracy: Financial and credit aspect. Public Policy And Administration, 19(3), 36–47. https://doi.org/10.5755/j01.ppaa.19.3.26842

Kumar, A. (2015). Criminalisation of Politics: Caste, Land and the State. India: Rawat Publications.

Kurlantzick, J. (2016). State Capitalism: How the Return of Statism is Transforming the World. Oxford University Press.

Lacroix, T. (2022). The transnational state and migration: Reach, flows and Policies. Political Geography, 94, 102571. https://doi.org/10.1016/j.polgeo.2021.102571

Lapavitsas, C. (2013). The financialisation of capitalism: 'Profiting without producing.' City, 17(6), 792–805. https://doi.org/10.1080/13604813.2013.853865

Laski, H. J. (2014). Studies in the problem of sovereignty (works of Harold J. Laski). Routledge.

Little, Kendall. (2021, June 11). Want to buy crypto? Here's what to look for in a crypto exchange. NextAdvisor.

Lokesh, K. (2020), Bad banks in India. Deloitte.

Lowenstein, L., Werner, W., & Smith, S. T. (1992). Is speculation "the essential native genius of the stock market"? Columbia Law Review, 92(1), 232. https://doi.org/10.2307/1123029

Maan, Jeet Singh (2019). International Journal of Transparency and accountability in governance. National Law University Delhi, Vol 5 UGC Care List ISSN 2395-4337

Mahurkar, U. (2018, May 10). Uday Mahurkar. India Today.

Maksimovic, L. M., Kostić, M., & Marjanović, G. (2019, March 1). RELATIONSHIP BETWEEN MODERN TRANSNATIONAL CORPORATIONS AND STATES: A VIEW OF DEVELOPING COUNTRIES. https://www.researchgate.net/publication/345309092_RELATIONSHIP_BETWEEN_MODERN_TRANSNATIONAL_CORPORATIONS_AND_STATES_A_VIEW_OF_DEVELOPING_COUNTRIES

Marina, A., Kuzmina, V. M., & Golo, A. A. (2020, May 11). Transnational corporations as actors of international relations. International Business Information Management Association (IBIMA). https://ibima.org/accepted-paper/transnational-corporations-as-actors-of-international-relations/

Martin, N., & Picherit, D. (2019). Special issue: Electoral fraud and manipulation in India and Pakistan. Commonwealth & Comparative Politics, 58(1), 1–20. https://doi.org/10.1080/14662043.2020.1700016

Maslin, M. (2013). Tectonics and climate. In Climate (pp. 61–78). Oxford University Press

Mason, P. (2016). PostCapitalism: A guide to our future. Penguin Books Limited.

MasterClass. (2021, November 18). Shell corporations explained: How shell corporations work - 2023. MasterClass. https://www.masterclass.com/articles/shell-corporation-explained

Mellor, M. (2010). The Future of Money: From financial crisis to public resource. Pluto Press

Mendel, Tony, et al. (2017) Concentration of Media Ownership and Freedom of Expression: Global Standards and Implications for the Americans. UNESCO, 2017, https://unesdoc.unesco.org/ark:/48223/pf0000248091.

Merriam, C. E. (1999). History of the theory of sovereignty since Rousseau. The Lawbook Exchange, Ltd.

Meyer, F. (2018, April). A shifting balance of power in world politics. ETH Zurich. https://ethz.ch/en/news-and-events/eth-news/news/2018/04/a-shifting-balance-of-power-in-world-politics.html

Mishra, P. (2018). Age of anger: A history of the present. Picador.

Moore & Hinckle, H. & M. (2020, November 3). Social media's impact on the 2020 presidential election: The good, the bad, and the ugly. Division of Research.

Mudde, C. (2000). The ideology of the extreme right. Manchester University Press. http://www.jstor.org/stable/j.ctt155j8h1

Mueller, T. J. (2015). *The coming new world order - The rise of global government* FriesenPress.

Mukherjee, D., Narasimha, V. L., Shukla, L., Mahadevan, J., Murthy, P., & Benegal, V. (2021). How do individuals with alcohol use disorders think about and respond to election dry days? Indian Journal of Psychological Medicine, 44(3), 313–315. https://doi.org/10.1177/02537176211013497

Nichols, S. (2019). Transnational Capital and the Transformation of the State: Investor-State Dispute Settlement (ISDS) in the Transatlantic Trade and Investment Partnership (TTIP). Critical Sociology, 45(1), 137–157. https://doi.org/10.1177/0896920516675205

Noam, E. M. (2009). The debate over media concentration and ownership. In Media Ownership and Concentration in America (pp. 3–25). Oxford University Press. http://dx.doi.org/10.1093/acprof:oso/9780195188523.003.0001

Noble, Barnes (2010). The New World Order: Facts & Fiction. Barnes & Noble, 2010.

Nollert, M. (2005). Transnational corporate ties: A synopsis of theories and empirical findings. Journal of World-Systems Research, 11(2), 289–314. https://doi.org/10.5195/jwsr.2005.383

OECD. (2001) 'Report on the Misuse of Corporate Vehicles for Illicit Purposes.' Behind the Corporate Veil using corporate entities for illicit purposes organisation for economic co-operation and development, 2001.

Pash, C. (2018, February 7). AMP has turned around its insurance business and is back in profit. Business Insider Australia.

Peterson-Withorn, C. (2021, April 6). Nearly 500 people became billionaires during the pandemic year. Forbes. https://www.forbes.com/sites/chasewithorn/2021/04/06/nearly-500-people-have-become-billionaires-during-the-pandemic-year/?sh=31f3b28725c0&utm_source=pocket_mylist

Pratap, V. (2021, March 10). In India, sedition law is the 'toolkit' to suppress dissent and criticism. The Print.

PTI. (2019, May 26). 43% of newly-elected Lok Sabha MPs have a criminal record: ADR. The Hindu.

Ravi, R. (2020, February 28). The Logical Indian. The Logical Indian.

Robinson. (2012, January 1). Global capitalism theory and the emergence of transnational elites. Palgrave Macmillan UK. https://link.springer.com/chapter/10.1057/9780230362406_3

Robinson. (2013). Social theory and globalisation: The rise of a transnational state. Theory and Society, 30(2), 157–200. https://doi.org/10.1023/A:1011077330455

Sampson, E.E. (1993). Identity politics: Challenges to psychology's understanding. American Psychologist, 48, 1219-1230.

Sawaya, Rubens R. (2019) Relations between State and Transnational Capital: The Case of Controls and Multipolarity. Geopolitical Economy Research Group. The Fourteenth Forum of the World Association for Political Economy 19-21 July 2019, the University of Manitoba, Winnipeg, Canada

Sawyer, M. C. (1988). Theories Of Monopoly Capitalism. Journal of Economic Surveys, 2(1), 47–76

Schmidt, V. A. (1995). The New World Order, Incorporated: The Rise of Business and the Decline of the Nation-State. Daedalus, 124(2), 75–106. http://www.jstor.org/stable/20027298

Scholtz, H. (2016, February 25). The future of world society. Hanno Scholtz - Academia.Edu. https://www.academia.edu/22464922/The_future_of_world_society

Seitz, K. (2019, August 8). UN signs a deal with Davos that threatens democratic principles. https://archive.globalpolicy.org/component/content/article/270-general/53120-un-signs-deal-with-davos-that-threatens-democratic-principles.html

Sharma, I., Vashnav, M., & Sharma, R. (2020). COVID-19 pandemic hype: Losers and gainers. Indian journal of psychiatry, 62(Suppl 3), S420–S430.

Shelanski, H. A. (2006). Antitrust law as mass media regulation: Can merger standards protect the public interest? California Law Review, 94(2), 371. https://doi.org/10.2307/20439038

Singh, S., Sharma, M. & Kaur, S. Eswar S. Prasad (2021): The future of money: how the digital revolution is transforming currencies and finance. J Evol Econ (2022). https://doi.org/10.1007/s00191-022-00774-7

Sismondo, S. (2017). Post-truth? Social Studies of Science, 47(1), 3–6. https://doi.org/10.1177/0306312717692076

Sklair, L. (2000). The transnational capitalist class and the discourse of globalisation. Cambridge Review of International Affairs, 14(1), 67–85. https://doi.org/10.1080/09557570008400329

SLAUGHTER, S. (2014). Transnational democratisation and republican citizenship: Towards critical republicanism. Global Constitutionalism, 3(3), 310-337. doi:10.1017/S2045381713000270

Spark, A. (2000). Conjuring Order: The New World Order and Conspiracy Theories of Globalisation. The Sociological Review, 48(2_suppl), 46–62.

Sprague, J. (2012). Transnational state. In The Wiley-Blackwell Encyclopaedia of Globalisation. John Wiley & Sons, Ltd.

Stasiulis, D., & Ross, D. (2006). Security, flexible sovereignty, and the perils of multiple citizenships. Citizenship Studies, 10(3), 329–348. https://doi.org/10.1080/13621020600772107

Štětka, V. (2010, January 1). Between a rock and a hard place? Market concentration, local ownership and media autonomy in the Czech Republic. Václav Štětka - Academia.Edu. https://www.academia.edu/7962829/Between_a_Rock_and_a_Hard_Place_Market_Concentration_Local_Ownership_and_Media_Autonomy_in_the_Czech_Republic

Sumption, J. (2022). Law in a time of crisis. Profile Books Ltd

Sweezy. (1990, January 1). Monopoly capitalism. Palgrave Macmillan UK. https://link.springer.com/chapter/10.1007/978-1-349-20572-1_44

Thomson, J. E. (1994). Mercenaries, Pirates, and Sovereigns: State-Building and Extraterritorial Violence in Early Modern Europe. Princeton University Press. http://www.jstor.org/stable/j.ctt7t30p

Uhlin, A. (1988). Transnational Corporations as Global Political Actors: A Literature Review. Cooperation and Conflict, 23(2), 231–247. https://doi.org/10.1177/001083678802300208

Uhlin, A. (1988). Transnational corporations as global political actors: A literature review. Cooperation and Conflict, 23(2), 231–247. https://doi.org/10.1177/001083678802300208

US Trade Representative. (2022). Transpacific Agreement. Https://Ustr.Gov/Trade-Agreements/Free-Trade-Agreements/Trans-Pacific-Partnership/Tpp-Full-Text. https://ustr.gov/trade-agreements/free-trade-agreements/trans-pacific-partnership/tpp-full-text

Vamaraju, N. (2019, March 11). Shelf companies & shell companies: 4 things to be aware of. Lawpath. https://lawpath.com.au/blog/shelf-companies-vs-shell-companies-4-things-you-should-be-aware-of

Van Cuilenburg, J. (1999). On Competition, Access and Diversity in Media, Old and New: Some Remarks for Communications Policy in the Information Age. New Media & Society, 1(2), 183–207. https://doi.org/10.1177/14614449922225555

Varadhan, S. (2022, June 29). India's top cement maker paying for Russian coal in Chinese yuan. The Wire. https://thewire.in/business/indias-top-cement-maker-paying-for-russian-coal-in-chinese-yuan

Wallerstein, I. (1974). The rise and future demise of the world capitalist system: Concepts for comparative analysis. Comparative Studies in Society and History, 16(4), 387–415. https://doi.org/10.2307/178015

Warner, M. (2017). Postcapitalism: A guide to our future; How will capitalism end?: Essays on a failing system; The perils of leaving economics to the experts; Inventing the future: Postcapitalism and a world without work. Asia Pacific Business Review, 24(1), 118–121. https://doi.org/10.1080/13602381.2017.1335511

Washburn, P.C. (1995). Democracy and media ownership: a comparison of commercial, public and government broadcast news. Media, Culture & Society, 17, 647 - 676.

Wecke, Ivan. (2021, August 24). Conspiracy theories aside, there is something fishy about the Great Reset. Resilience. https://www.resilience.org/stories/2021-08-24/conspiracy-theories-aside-there-is-something-fishy-about-the-great-reset/

William Outhwaite. (2008) The Future of Society. John Wiley & Sons.

Yalcin, O. G. (2019, January 1). Taxation of cryptocurrencies and initial coin offerings. Orhan Gazi Yalcin - Academia.Edu. https://www.academia.edu/44158568/Taxation_of_Cryptocurrencies_and_Initial_Coin_Offerings

Zekos, P. A. (1989). The Corporate Republic: Economics of Power. ABC Books. (Original work published 1989)

About the Author

Entrepreneur, thought leader, writer, and social activist Balvinder Ruby is the author of "The Provocateur: Spilling Beans, by all means", an ensemble of inspirational, motivational, and uplifting poems.

Balvinder has contributed to and is a Brand Ambassador of "The Times of India", the largest English daily newspaper of India, in Sydney.

He is an Earth Scientist and a researcher by qualifications and training and has worked for over two decades in that capacity.

You can connect with me on

Web: https://balvinderruby.com.au

Also by Balvinder Ruby

The Provocateur: Spilling beans by all means by Balvinder Ruby

The Provocateur: Spilling beans, by all means, is a fully illustrated compilation of 38 motivational, inspirational and uplifting poems. Individual poems have a theme and have been thematically presented with black and white pencil sketches.

This book intends to walk you through the length and breadth of your mindscape, arouse curiosity, invoke intellect and provoke you to reflect and realise your full potential to enable you to cruise the mundane daily grind harmoniously.

It seeks to dislodge you from your comfort zone, kick your butt, unsettle and prod you to start grappling for your grit to get you thinking to the barge and take charge.

It is also directed to enrage you to engage and manage the stage, restrain from blaming others, align yourself with your real authentic self and claim, seek and fight for your right without any insinuations and position yourself at the crossroads to decide for yourself whether and whither to here from and henceforth.

What others say

"an extraordinary piece of writing, intelligent and very reflective"

– Adjunct Professor Dr Jim Taggart, OAM,
Deputy Chairman Riverside Theatres

www.ingramcontent.com/pod-product-compliance
Lightning Source LLC
Chambersburg PA
CBHW071710020426
42333CB00017B/2202